国家社科基金重点项目"中国古代蒙学典籍的海外传播及其影响研究"(17AZS012)、全球中文教育主题学术活动资助计划项目"新时期中文国际传播体系研究"(SH20Y18)、国家语委"十四五"科研规划2021年度委托项目"国际中文教育标准体系框架研究"(WT145-2)成果

One-Thousand-Character Essay

中国古代蒙学典籍双语多功能系列教材

任晓霏 张 杰 袁 礼 主编

东南大学出版社

·南京·

内 容 提 要

本书分为24课,在《千字文》原文基础上通过话题讨论引入课文学习,通过拼音、汉字、语法知识学习、口语练习等方式帮助学习者在较好地理解原文的基础上学习语言知识。每一课的延伸学习还能帮助学习者初步了解与课文主题相关的文化背景知识。

本书既可用于汉语国际教育专业学位研究生的中华文化传播实践课程,也可用于海外孔子学院(课堂)等中文教育课程,同时也适用于国内中小学生的"蒙学"课程。

图书在版编目(CIP)数据

千字文 / 任晓霏,张杰,袁礼主编. — 南京:东南大学出版社,2022.9
 ISBN 978-7-5766-0219-7

Ⅰ.①千… Ⅱ.①任… ②张… ③袁… Ⅲ.①古汉语-启蒙读物 Ⅳ.①H194.1

中国版本图书馆 CIP 数据核字(2022)第 152321 号

责任编辑:刘 坚　　责任校对:周 菊　　封面设计:余武莉　　责任印制:周荣虎

千字文　Qianziwen

主　　编	任晓霏 张 杰 袁 礼
出版发行	东南大学出版社
社　　址	南京市四牌楼2号(邮编:210096 电话:025-83793330)
经　　销	全国各地新华书店
印　　刷	江苏凤凰数码印务有限公司
开　　本	787mm×1092mm　1/16
印　　张	16.5
字　　数	390 千字
版　　次	2022年9月第1版
印　　次	2022年9月第1次印刷
书　　号	ISBN 978-7-5766-0219-7
定　　价	68.00 元

本社图书若有印装质量问题,请直接与营销部调换。电话(传真):025-83791830

  本书是国家社科基金重点项目"中国古代蒙学典籍的海外传播及其影响研究"(17AZS012)、全球中文教育主题学术活动资助计划项目"新时期中文国际传播体系研究"(SH20Y18)、国家语委"十四五"科研规划2021年度委托项目"国际中文教育标准体系框架研究"(WT145－2)成果,也是江苏大学研究生教材建设专项的成果。

  中国政府历来重视中华优秀传统文化的传承发展,始终从中华民族最深沉精神追求的深度看待优秀传统文化,从国家战略资源的高度继承优秀传统文化,从推动中华民族现代化进程的角度创新发展优秀传统文化,使之成为实现"两个一百年"奋斗目标和中华民族伟大复兴中国梦的根本性力量。深入挖掘中华优秀传统文化蕴含的思想观念、人文精神、道德规范,结合时代要求继承创新,让中华文化展现出永久魅力和时代风采;让世界知道"为人类文明作贡献的中国",是时代赋予学人的一项光荣而艰巨的任务。

  语言是沟通交流的桥梁和纽带。当前,"中文热"持续升温,越来越多的国家将中文纳入国民教育体系,各国对学习中文的需求持续旺盛,汉语人才越来越受到欢迎。国务院副总理孙春兰在2019国际中文教育大会开幕式致辞中强调,中国政府把推动国际中文教育作为义不容辞的责任,积极发挥汉语母语国的优势,在师资、教材、课程等方面创造条件,为各国民众学习中文提供支持。我们将遵循语言传播的国际惯例,按照相互尊重、友好协商、平等互利的原则,坚持市场化运作,支持中外高校、企业、社会组织开展国际中文教育项目和交流合作,聚焦语言主业,适应本土需求,帮助当地培养中文教育人才,完善国际中文教育标准,发挥汉语水平考试的评价导向作用,构建更加开放、包容、规范的现代国际中文教育体系。

  中国古代蒙学发轫于殷周,秦汉时期得到迅速发展,唐宋年间已经十分成熟,明清时期更是达到鼎盛。中国古代蒙学典籍所承载的汉字文化使华夏文明历久弥新,绵延不绝,并在数千年的发展历程中辐射周边,推进了汉字文化圈的形成,进而远播欧美,使儒家思想给西方现代文明带来了曙光。历代蒙学传承中华文明,并在中外文化交流史上,先后在汉字文化圈和欧美文化圈得到广泛传播,为世界文明的发展和进步注入了东方智慧。

中国传统蒙学典籍历史悠久,文化积淀深厚,是中华文明体系中语言、文化传承与传播的重要载体。让学习者通过蒙学典籍领略汉字文化的魅力,传承和传播中华优秀文化,具有十分重要的学术意义和社会价值。

蒙学最惊人之处是其蒙学教材。中国传统蒙学教材内容丰富,包罗万象,常简称为蒙学"三百千千弟子规"(《三字经》《百家姓》《千字文》《千家诗》《弟子规》),其中又以"三(字经)、百(家姓)、千(字文)"最为知名。蒙学教材使用时间之长、范围之广空前绝后,足可以载入"吉尼斯世界纪录"。张志公1992年在《传统语文教育教材论——暨蒙学书目和书影》中对古代蒙学教材做了极为详尽的考证,编订了《蒙学书目》。他把古代蒙学教材分为21类,收录近600种蒙学书籍,为蒙学研究提供了宝贵的参考资料。较有名的蒙学教材见下表:

表1　重要蒙学教材列表

《三字经》	《百家姓》	《千字文》	《千家诗》
《小儿语》	《弟子规》	《五字鉴》	《增广贤文》
《小学诗》	《龙文鞭影》	《朱子家训》	《笠翁对韵》
《名贤集》	《幼学琼林》	《蒙求》	《唐诗三百首》
《格言联璧》	《声律启蒙》	《二十四孝》	《训蒙骈句》
《小学绀珠》	《急就篇》	《太公家教》	《小学》
《史籀篇》	《仓颉》	《蒙养故事》	《颜氏家训》

在推进国家社科基金重点项目的研究工作中,我们发现,中国古代蒙学典籍在国际中文教学史上作为汉语教材发挥了重要作用;但在近代的影响逐渐式微。在新时期推进传统优秀文化的创造性转化与创新性发展进程中,我们计划面向国际中文教育领域推出"中国古代蒙学典籍双语多功能系列教程",为海内外汉语学习者提供理解汉字本真、掌握汉语韵律、学好汉语语言的传统经典教材。

"中国古代蒙学典籍双语多功能系列教材"正是以传承与传播中华优秀传统文化为宗旨,以高等教育国际化为平台,以新媒体技术为依托,深入挖掘、阐发蒙学典籍所蕴含的汉字文化精髓和人类共同价值,为推进"一带一路"倡议和人类命运共同体构建做出努力,为构建新时期中国语言文化全球传播体系做出有益探索。

《千字文》是中国历代蒙学典籍中的首选教材,是中国影响力极大的儿童启蒙读物。梁武帝萧衍(464—549)是一位文学素养极高的文人皇帝,为了让皇室子弟学好书法,特命文学侍从殷铁石从王羲之作品中拓出了一千个不同的字;后又请当时的文学奇才散骑侍郎、给事中周兴嗣谱写成便于记诵的韵文。周兴嗣将其编成了一篇由250句、1000个汉字组成的韵文。《千字文》通篇皆为四字句,对仗工整,条理清晰,文采斐然,易诵易记。据传说,周兴嗣为此一夜白头。中国实行简化字、归并异体字后,其简体中文版本剩下九百九十余个相异汉字。现有英文版、法文版、拉丁文版、意大利文版等译本。

《千字文》中字与字的排列组合呈现出深厚的文化底蕴和人文内涵,内容包含天文地理、历史经典、伦理道德,具有深厚的哲学和文学意蕴,蕴含儒家"仁""义""礼""智""信"等价值观。通过学习,可以帮助海内外汉语学习者深入了解中国优秀传统文化,深刻领会汉字精髓。由于时代的局限性,其中的某些思想或观点,如四大五常等,已经过时陈旧或不符合当代价值观,我们应该有选择地批判学习。有些汉字现在已经过时或比较生僻,学习者只需要认识即可。

通过本教材的学习,我们希望:(1) 实现蒙学典籍的创造性转化和创新型发展,使中国传统蒙学经典焕发新生;(2) 以汉字文化为重点,弘扬中华优秀文化,推进国际中文教育;(3) 培养留学生"知华友华"情怀,助推"一带一路"建设,为推进构建"人类命运共同体"做出有益探索。

该教程具有三个主要特色:

(1) 英汉双语。为了有效推进蒙学典籍的国际传播,教材以英汉双语为教学媒介。

(2) 多功能。教材编写既有核心汉字的解读,又有汉字文化知识的普及,还有相关历史故事的阐述,有利于扩大教材的适用范围,满足中外学生的多种学习功能。

(3) 新媒体技术。引入二维码、移动终端技术,实现经典教材的空间立体化呈现,提升经典教材的现代性和智能化。

《千字文》的中文释义遵循"简明准确"的原则,教材最后附编者的英文译本,可以帮助学生理解原文。本教材注重学生理解,每课以话题讨论引入,从不同文化思想碰撞到中国传统典籍学习,再到课后口语练习,每课首尾呼应,重任务型学习,以学生对中国文化的理解与评价为重点,关注学生的汉语输出和表达能力。从蒙学经典到日常交际,由古至今,从文化源头到现实生活,开阔学生视野,联系生活实际,在学习中国优秀传统文化的同时,与当代中国社会和文化相衔接。

本教材既可应用于汉语国际教育专业学位研究生的中华文化传播实

践课程,也可以适用于海外大学中文系(专业)、孔子学院、孔子课堂等国际中文教育机构的汉字教学,还可作为在华国际学生中文学习教材,也可供海外汉学家和具有一定中文基础(已经通过或达到 HSK 2 级)的国际学生研究参考,同时,还可作为国内中小学生的课外阅读教材。

本书由江苏大学文学院任晓霏、张杰和中外语言交流合作中心袁礼担任主编,任晓霏教授指导的硕士研究生参与教材编写工作。其中任晓霏、袁礼负责教材的研究统筹、理念设计和文字统稿,张杰负责教材编写的组织管理、英文翻译和统稿;李红艳老师负责中文审校;钟维、刘妍汝和杨茗负责各小组的分工、协调和统稿。各课初稿的编写分工如下:1—4 课,钟维、张雨昕、尹思纯、邹国栋;5—8 课,刘妍汝、曹霞、刘胜男;9—12 课,胡晗、汪可、杨茗;13—16 课,尤磊、周楚越、沙博翰;17—20 课,王丹迪、李巧、张雅雯。初稿校对由钟维(1—4 课)、刘妍汝(5—8 课)、胡晗(9—12 课)、尤磊(13—16 课)、王丹迪(17—20 课)负责。初稿完工后,2021 年 3 月教育部发布新版《国际中文教育中文水平等级标准》(2021 年 7 月 1 日起实施)。我们及时根据新标准对教材内容进行了更新调整,第二稿具体分工如下:沙博翰,1、21 课;周楚越,2、8 课;张雅雯,3、11 课;尹思纯,4、24 课;邹国栋,5、10 课;刘胜男,6、14 课;杨茗,7、9 课;汪可,12 课;李士凤,13 课;濮凤娇,15 课;金艺萌,16 课;李巧,17、18 课;晏明丽,19 课;朱慧妍,20 课;赵淑婷,22 课;尤晨玮,23 课。

由于编写人员水平有限,教材难免存在错误、疏漏和不足之处,恳请方家批评指正并不吝赐教,以便我们进一步改进工作。

本书附有音频,可扫码下载或播放。

编写组
2022 年 4 月

常用汉英语法术语

Common Chinese-English Grammatical Terms

被动语态	passive voice	不定冠词	indefinite article
不及物动词	intransitive verb	不可数名词	uncountable noun
陈述句	declarative sentence	词性	part of speech
搭配	collocation	代词	pronoun
定冠词	definite article	动词	verb
复合句	compound sentence	复杂句	complex sentence
副词	adverb	感叹词	interjection
感叹句	exclamatory sentence	冠词	article
及物动词	transitive verb	简单句	simple sentence
介词	preposition	句法	syntax
句型	sentence pattern	可数名词	countable noun
连词	conjunction	名词	noun
情态动词	modal verb	时态	tense
实词	content word	数词	numeral
形容词	adjective	虚词	function word
疑问句	interrogative sentence	语法	grammar
语气词	modal particle	语态	voice
主动语态	active voice	助词	auxiliary

人物简介

王老师:专职汉语教师,40岁,主讲中国古代蒙学课程。

李华:巴基斯坦人,22岁,HSK 3级,来中国学习汉语一年,性格开朗,有很多中国朋友,对中国传统文化感兴趣。

张丽丽:俄罗斯人,25岁,HSK 3级,来中国学习汉语一年,与李华为同一语言班同学,学习刻苦努力,想要成为一名汉语老师。

刘芳:英国人,27岁,HSK 3级,来中国5年,曾为跨国企业员工,在中国工作4年,在工作中接触汉语,喜欢中华文化,后进入大学学习汉语。

陈士杰:泰国人,24岁,HSK 3级,来中国学习汉语半年,想成为导游。

Characters

Professor WANG: TCSOL professor, 40, specialized in teaching ancient Chinese primers.

LI Hua: Pakistani, 22, HSK-3, having studied Chinese for one year in China, outgoing, sociable, interested in traditional Chinese culture.

ZHANG Lili: Russian, 25, HSK-3, having studied Chinese for one year in China, Li Hua's classmate, diligent, aspiring to be a Chinese teacher.

LIU Fang: British, 27, HSK-3, 5 years in China (an MNC employee for 4 years), having a craze for Chinese culture, currently studying Chinese at college.

CHEN Shijie: Thai, 24, HSK-3, having studied Chinese for 6 months in China, desiring to be a tourist guide.

第一课　天地玄黄 Lesson One　Dark Sky and Yellow Earth

　　一、课前练习（Warm-up） ………………………………… 001

　　二、学习原文（Text） ……………………………………… 002

　　三、汉字学习（Chinese character） ……………………… 003

　　四、日常对话（Dialogue） ………………………………… 007

　　五、语法知识（Grammar） ………………………………… 008

　　六、课后练习（Exercises） ………………………………… 008

　　七、延伸学习（Extended reading） ……………………… 010

第二课　金生丽水 Lesson Two　Gold from the Bottom of the Jinsha River

　　一、课前练习（Warm-up） ………………………………… 011

　　二、学习原文（Text） ……………………………………… 012

　　三、汉字学习（Chinese character） ……………………… 013

　　四、日常对话（Dialogue） ………………………………… 016

　　五、语法知识（Grammar） ………………………………… 017

　　六、课后练习（Exercises） ………………………………… 017

　　七、延伸学习（Extended learning） ……………………… 019

第三课　龙师火帝 Lesson Three　Fuxi and Shennong

　　一、课前练习（Warm-up） ………………………………… 020

　　二、学习原文（Text） ……………………………………… 021

　　三、汉字学习（Chinese character） ……………………… 021

四、日常对话（Dialogue） ……………………………………… 023
　　五、语法知识（Grammar） ……………………………………… 024
　　六、课后练习（Exercises） ……………………………………… 025
　　七、延伸学习（Extended reading） …………………………… 026

第四课　坐朝问道　Lesson Four　Governing a State

　　一、课前练习（Warm-up） ……………………………………… 027
　　二、学习原文（Text） …………………………………………… 028
　　三、汉字学习（Chinese character） …………………………… 029
　　四、日常对话（Dialogue） ……………………………………… 032
　　五、语法知识（Grammar） ……………………………………… 032
　　六、课后练习（Exercises） ……………………………………… 033
　　七、延伸学习（Extended reading） …………………………… 034

第五课　盖此身发　Lesson Five　Self-cultivation

　　一、课前练习（Warm-up） ……………………………………… 035
　　二、学习原文（Text） …………………………………………… 036
　　三、汉字学习（Chinese character） …………………………… 037
　　四、日常对话（Dialogue） ……………………………………… 041
　　五、语法知识（Grammar） ……………………………………… 042
　　六、课后练习（Exercises） ……………………………………… 043
　　七、延伸学习（Extended reading） …………………………… 044

第六课　景行维贤　Lesson Six　Virtuous People and Philosophers

　　一、课前练习（Warm-up） ……………………………………… 045
　　二、学习原文（Text） …………………………………………… 046
　　三、汉字学习（Chinese character） …………………………… 047
　　四、日常对话（Dialogue） ……………………………………… 052
　　五、语法知识（Grammar） ……………………………………… 052

六、课后练习（Exercises） ……………………………… 053
七、延伸学习（Extended reading） ……………………… 054

| 第七课 资父事君 | Lesson Seven Waiting on Your Father and Serving Your King |

一、课前练习（Warm-up） ………………………………… 056
二、学习原文（Text） ……………………………………… 057
三、汉字学习（Chinese character） ……………………… 058
四、日常对话（Dialogue） ………………………………… 062
五、语法知识（Grammar） ………………………………… 063
六、课后练习（Exercises） ………………………………… 063
七、延伸练习（Extended reading） ……………………… 065

| 第八课 容止若思 | Lesson Eight Be Self-collected and Behave Prudently |

一、课前练习（Warm-up） ………………………………… 066
二、学习原文（Text） ……………………………………… 067
三、汉字学习（Chinese character） ……………………… 068
四、日常对话（Dialogue） ………………………………… 073
五、语法知识（Grammar） ………………………………… 074
六、课后练习（Exercises） ………………………………… 075
七、延伸练习（Extended Reading） ……………………… 076

| 第九课 乐殊贵贱 | Lesson Nine Different Music for Different People |

一、课前练习（Warm-up） ………………………………… 077
二、学习原文（Text） ……………………………………… 078
三、汉字学习（Chinese character） ……………………… 079
四、日常对话（Dialogue） ………………………………… 083
五、语法知识（Grammar） ………………………………… 084
六、课后练习（Exercises） ………………………………… 085
七、延伸学习（Extended reading） ……………………… 086

第十课 仁慈隐恻 Lesson Ten　Mercy and Sympathy

一、课前练习（Warm-up） ·· 087

二、学习原文（Text） ··· 088

三、汉字学习（Chinese character） ······························· 089

四、日常对话（Dialogue） ·· 092

五、语法知识（Grammar） ·· 092

六、课后练习（Exercises） ······································· 093

七、延伸学习（Extended reading） ································ 094

第十一课 都邑华夏 Lesson Eleven　Magnificent Ancient Capitals

一、课前练习（Warm-up） ·· 095

二、学习原文（Text） ··· 096

三、汉字学习（Chinese character） ······························· 096

四、日常对话（Dialogue） ·· 099

五、语法知识（Grammar） ·· 100

六、课后练习（Exercises） ······································· 100

七、延伸学习（Extended reading） ································ 101

第十二课 肆筵设席 Lesson Twelve　Banquet and Music

一、课前练习（Warm-up） ·· 103

二、学习原文（Text） ··· 104

三、汉字学习（Chinese character） ······························· 104

四、日常对话（Dialogue） ·· 109

五、语法知识（Grammar） ·· 110

六、课后练习（Exercises） ······································· 111

七、延伸学习（Extended reading） ································ 112

第十三课 府罗将相　Lesson Thirteen　Generals and Ministers

一、课前练习（Warm-up） ……………………………………… 114

二、学习原文（Text） …………………………………………… 115

三、汉字学习（Chinese character） …………………………… 116

四、日常对话（Dialogue） ……………………………………… 119

五、语法知识（Grammar） ……………………………………… 120

六、课后练习（Exercises） ……………………………………… 120

七、延伸学习（Extended reading） …………………………… 122

第十四课 磻溪伊尹　Lesson Fourteen　Jiang Ziya and Yi Yin

一、课前练习（Warm-up） ……………………………………… 123

二、学习原文（Text） …………………………………………… 124

三、汉字学习（Chinese character） …………………………… 125

四、日常对话（Dialogue） ……………………………………… 129

五、语法知识（Grammar） ……………………………………… 129

六、课后练习（Exercises） ……………………………………… 130

七、延伸学习（Extended reading） …………………………… 131

第十五课 晋楚更霸　Lesson Fifteen　Jin Superseding Chu

一、课前练习（Warm-up） ……………………………………… 133

二、学习原文（Text） …………………………………………… 134

三、汉字学习（Chinese character） …………………………… 135

四、日常对话（Dialogue） ……………………………………… 139

五、语法知识（Grammar） ……………………………………… 140

六、课后练习（Exercises） ……………………………………… 140

七、延伸学习（Extended reading） …………………………… 141

第十六课　九州禹迹　Lesson Sixteen　Footprints of Dayu in Ancient China

　　一、课前练习（Warm-up） ……………………………… 143
　　二、学习原文（Text） …………………………………… 144
　　三、汉字学习（Chinese character） …………………… 145
　　四、日常对话（Dialogue） ……………………………… 146
　　五、语法知识（Grammar） ……………………………… 148
　　六、课后练习（Exercises） ……………………………… 148
　　七、延伸学习（Extended reading） …………………… 149

第十七课　治本于农　Lesson Seventeen　Agriculture, Foundation of a Country

　　一、课前练习（Warm-up） ……………………………… 151
　　二、学习原文（Text） …………………………………… 152
　　三、汉字学习（Chinese character） …………………… 152
　　四、日常对话（Dialogue） ……………………………… 155
　　五、语法知识（Grammar） ……………………………… 156
　　六、课后练习（Exercises） ……………………………… 156
　　七、延伸学习（Extended reading） …………………… 158

第十八课　聆音察理　Lesson Eighteen　Hearing the Sound and Telling the Truth

　　一、课前练习（Warm-up） ……………………………… 159
　　二、学习原文（Text） …………………………………… 160
　　三、汉字学习（Chinese character） …………………… 161
　　四、日常对话（Dialogue） ……………………………… 164
　　五、语法知识（Grammar） ……………………………… 165
　　六、课后练习（Exercises） ……………………………… 166
　　七、延伸学习（Extended reading） …………………… 167

| 第十九课　求古寻论 | Lesson Nineteen　Exploring the Ancients and Reading Some Famous Quotes |

　　一、课前练习（Warm-up）·················· 169

　　二、学习原文（Text）······················· 170

　　三、汉字学习（Chinese character）·········· 171

　　四、日常对话（Dialogue）··················· 175

　　五、语法知识（Grammar）··················· 177

　　六、课后练习（Exercises）·················· 177

　　七、延伸学习（Extended reading）··········· 179

| 第二十课　耽读玩市 | Lesson Twenty　Indulging in Reading in the Market |

　　一、课前练习（Warm-up）·················· 180

　　二、学习原文（Text）······················· 181

　　三、汉字学习（Chinese character）·········· 182

　　四、日常对话（Dialogue）··················· 185

　　五、语法知识（Grammar）··················· 185

　　六、课后练习（Exercises）·················· 186

　　七、延伸学习（Extended reading）··········· 187

| 第二十一课　妾御绩纺 | Lesson Twenty-one　Concubines and Servants Should Do the Housework |

　　一、课前练习（Warm-up）·················· 189

　　二、学习原文（Text）······················· 190

　　三、汉字学习（Chinese character）·········· 191

　　四、日常对话（Dialogue）··················· 194

　　五、语法知识（Grammar）··················· 195

　　六、课后练习（Exercises）·················· 195

　　七、延伸学习（Extended reading）··········· 197

第二十二课 嫡后嗣续 Lesson Twenty-two Descendants and Inheritance

    一、课前练习（Warm-up） ······················· 198
    二、学习原文（Text） ···························· 199
    三、汉字学习（Chinese character） ··············· 200
    四、日常对话（Dialogue） ······················· 202
    五、语法知识（Grammar） ························ 202
    六、课后练习（Exercises） ······················· 203
    七、延伸学习（Extended learning） ··············· 204

第二十三课 诛斩贼盗 Lesson Twenty-three Eradication of Thieves and Bandits

    一、课前练习（Warm-up） ······················· 206
    二、学习原文（Text） ···························· 207
    三、汉字学习（Chinese character） ··············· 208
    四、日常对话（Dialogue） ······················· 211
    五、语法知识（Grammar） ························ 212
    六、课后练习（Exercises） ······················· 212
    七、延伸学习（Extended reading） ··············· 214

第二十四课 年矢每催 Lesson Twenty-four Time Pressing Forward

    一、课前练习（Warm-up） ······················· 215
    二、学习原文（Text） ···························· 216
    三、汉字学习（Chinese character） ··············· 217
    四、日常对话（Dialogue） ······················· 219
    五、语法知识（Grammar） ························ 220
    六、课后练习（Exercises） ······················· 221
    七、延伸学习（Extended Reading） ··············· 222

附录一　生字表 ···································· 223
附录二　练习参考答案 ······························ 226
附录三　本教材中华典籍汉英对照表 ··················· 230
附录四　One-Thousand-Character Essay ··············· 232

第一课　天地玄黄

Lesson One　Dark Sky and Yellow Earth

 课前练习 Warm-up

1. 描红并注音(Trace strokes and add pinyin)

2. 话题导入(Topic introduction)

说说你眼中的天空是什么颜色的？
What color is the sky in your eyes?

Tiān dì xuán① huáng, yǔ zhòu hóng huāng。
天　地　玄　黄，宇　宙　洪　荒。

Rì yuè yíng② zè③, chén xiù④ liè zhāng。
日　月　盈　昃，辰　宿　列　张。

Hán lái shǔ wǎng, qiū shōu dōng cáng。
寒　来　暑　往，秋　收　冬　藏。

Rùn⑤ yú chéng suì, lǜ lǚ⑥ tiáo yáng。
闰　余　成　岁，律　吕　调　阳。

Yún téng zhì yǔ, lù jié wéi shuāng。
云　腾　致　雨，露　结　为　霜。

1. 注释(Notes)

①玄：黑色，苍天的颜色（black）。

②盈：月光饱满（full moon），指月亮圆。

③昃：太阳偏西（the sun in the west）。

④宿：中国古代指天空中某些星的集合体（names of some constellations in ancient China）。

⑤闰：闰年（leap year）。

⑥律吕：中国古代礼乐中的规则、标准（rules and standards in the ancient Chinese system of rites and music）。

2. 原文大意(Paraphrase)

黑色的上天，黄色的大地；宇宙在混沌蒙昧中渐渐成形，宇宙无边无际。
太阳起起落落，月亮圆圆缺缺；星星散布在夜空中，满天星辰排列有序。
冬夏循环变换，四季不停更替；秋天收割庄稼，冬天储藏粮食。
数年的闰余积累成一个月，放在闰年里；古人用六律六吕来调节阴阳。
水汽上升遇冷形成雨，露水遇冷结成霜。

三 汉字学习 Chinese character

第一课 天地玄黄

宇

拼音	yǔ
词性	名词（n.）
释义	空间（space）；房屋（house）
搭配	宇宙（universe）
例句	宇宙无边无际。The universe is boundless.

洪

拼音	hóng
词性	名词（n.）
释义	大水（flood）
搭配	洪水（flood）
例句	洪水冲倒了很多房子。 The flood washed down many houses.

辰

拼音	chén
词性	名词（n.）
释义	时光（time）
搭配	诞辰（birthday）
例句	今天是李小龙的诞辰，我们在此纪念他。 Today is Bruce Lee's birthday and we are here to commemorate him.

宿

拼音	xiù；sù

003

词性	名词(n.)；动词(v.)
释义	星座（constellation）；留（stay）
搭配	星宿（constellation）；宿舍（dormitory）
例句	学校留学生宿舍的条件很好。 The university's international student dormitory is in good condition.

拼音	liè
词性	动词(v.)
释义	按顺序展示(display in order)
搭配	陈列(display)
例句	博物馆里陈列着这群人的两张珍贵的合影。 Two precious photographs of the group are on display in the museum.

拼音	zhāng
词性	动词(v.)
释义	打开(open)
搭配	紧张(nervous)
例句	快考试了,他看上去很紧张。 It's almost exam time and he looks very nervous.

拼音	hán
词性	形容词(adj.)
释义	冷的(cold)

搭配	寒假(winter holiday);严寒(severe cold)
例句	他开始了来中国后的第一个寒假生活。 He started his first winter holiday in China.

拼音	shǔ
词性	形容词(adj.)
释义	炎热的(hot)
搭配	暑假(summer holiday)
例句	暑假,我复习了中文。 During the summer holiday, I reviewed my Chinese.

拼音	cáng
词性	动词(v.)
释义	保存(save)
搭配	收藏(collect)
例句	他喜欢收藏邮票。 He likes collecting stamps.

拼音	yú
词性	形容词(adj.)
释义	剩下的(left)

搭配	多余的(surplus)
例句	这里没有多余的座位了。No more seats here.

律 ノ 彳 彳 彳 彳 彳 律 律 律

拼音	lǜ
词性	名词(n.)
释义	标准(standard)；规则(rule)
搭配	法律(law)；律师(lawyer)
例句	她是一位非常成功的律师。 She is a very successful lawyer.

调 ` 讠 讠 讠 讠 调 调 调 调

拼音	tiáo
词性	动词(v.)
释义	使搭配均匀；使协和(make the collocation even and harmonious)
搭配	调和(harmonize)；协调(coordinate, match)
例句	我看得出来有些颜色不协调。 I can see that some colors cannot match each other.

致 一 丁 互 至 至 至 至 致 致

拼音	zhì
词性	动词(v.)
释义	引起(lead to)
搭配	导致(cause)
例句	粗心导致他今天没赶上公交车。 He missed the bus because of his carelessness today.

露

拼音	lù
词性	名词(*n.*)；动词(*v.*)
释义	早晨的水珠(dew)；显现(expose)
搭配	流露(reveal, spread)；揭露(disclose)
例句	他脸上露出开心的笑容。 A happy smile spread across his face.

日常对话 Dialogue

（一）新学期（The new semester）

李　华：好久不见，丽丽！你放假去旅行了吗？

张丽丽：好久不见！我坐高铁去了北京。

李　华：你为什么不坐飞机？

张丽丽：因为我想看看路上的风景，所以坐高铁，而且高铁速度很快，很方便。你去旅行了吗？

李　华：没有，我回家了，所以没有去旅行。

张丽丽：那也很好，你可以跟家人在一起。

（二）《千字文》（*One-Thousand-Character Essay*）

刘　芳：这学期我们学习《千字文》，我很激动。

陈士杰：我也是。听说《千字文》就是一千个汉字写

千字文

chéng de hěn lì hai
成 的，很 厉 害！

Liú Fāng: Shì de! Ér qiě shì yì qiān gè bù tóng de hàn zì.
刘 芳：是的！而 且 是 一 千 个 不 同 的 汉 字。

Chén Shì jié: Duì, xué le wǒ men jiù huì yì qiān gè hàn zì le.
陈 士 杰：对，学 了 我 们 就 会 一 千 个 汉 字 了。

Liú Fāng: Shì a, ér qiě wǒ tīng shuō tā bù nán!
刘 芳：是 啊，而 且 我 听 说 它 不 难！

Chén Shì jié: Zhēn de ma? Tài hǎo le!
陈 士 杰：真 的 吗？太 好 了！

五 语法知识 Grammar

1. 疑问句(为什么)

用法：询问原因。

句型：主语＋为什么＋动词＋名词。

例句：你为什么学中文？

你为什么来中国？

2. 连词(而且)

用法：表示递进。

句型：描述1＋而且＋描述2。

例句：高铁速度很快，而且很方便。

李华会说中文，而且说得很好。

六 课后练习 Exercises

1. 写一写(Writing)

根据拼音写汉字。

Write down the corresponding characters according to pinyin.

  lù   shǔ   zhǐ   tiáo

法＿＿＿＿ ＿＿＿＿假 导＿＿＿＿ ＿＿＿＿和

2．连一连(Matching)

把右列的汉字与左列的汉字相连组词。

Match characters in the right column with one in the left column to form a phrase.

陈　　　　　　　　　寒
阳　　　　　　　　　余
严　　　　　　　　　露
收　　　　　　　　　列
流　　　　　　　　　光
多　　　　　　　　　藏

3．填一填(Blank-filling)

用课文中的汉字填空。

Fill the following blanks with characters in the text.

(1) 他脸上＿＿＿＿出开心的笑容。

(2) 快考试了,他看上去很紧＿＿＿＿。

(3) 红色和绿色在一起很不协＿＿＿＿。

(4) 他喜欢收＿＿＿＿邮票。

4．默一默(Writing from memory)

根据课文内容填空。

Fill in the blanks according to the text.

日月盈昃,辰宿＿＿＿＿张。

＿＿＿＿来＿＿＿＿往,秋＿＿＿＿冬藏。

5．说一说(Talking)

根据所给场景,编写对话并练习。

Based on the given situations, make dialogues and practice.

这个假期你去旅游了吗? 说一说你在假期做了什么?

＿＿＿＿＿＿＿＿＿＿＿＿＿＿＿＿＿＿＿＿＿＿＿＿＿＿＿＿

＿＿＿＿＿＿＿＿＿＿＿＿＿＿＿＿＿＿＿＿＿＿＿＿＿＿＿＿

＿＿＿＿＿＿＿＿＿＿＿＿＿＿＿＿＿＿＿＿＿＿＿＿＿＿＿＿

千字文

《千字文》简介

《千字文》是中国古代影响深远的儿童启蒙读物,是由南北朝时期梁朝的周兴嗣(469—537)编写的,由一千个汉字组成。梁武帝(464—549)命人从王羲之(303—361,书法家)的书法作品中选取1 000个不重复的汉字,命员外散骑侍郎周兴嗣编写成文。全文为四字句,对仗工整,条理清晰。《千字文》的语言简单通俗,易诵易记,已被翻译为英文、法文、拉丁文、意大利文等其他语言。

文中1 000个字本来没有重复,但周兴嗣在编写文章时,用了"洁""絜"这两个同义异体字。中国简化汉字后,其简体中文版本剩下九百九十余个相异汉字。

One-Thousand-Character Essay〔千(qian, thousand)字(zi, character)文(wen, essay)〕has been exerting a great influence on children's enlightenment reading since the Southern and Northern Dynasties in China. Under the order of Emperor Liang Wudi (464 – 549), Zhou Xingsi(469 – 537) selected 1,000 different Chinese characters from the calligraphy works of Wang Xizhi(303 – 361), the well-known calligrapher, and compiled them into an essay. The full text is made up of four-character sentences with neat and clear organization. The language of *One-Thousand-Character Essay* is simple and popular, easy to recite and remember. It has been translated into English, French, Latin, Italian and many other languages.

There were no repeated Chinese characters in the original *One-Thousand-Character Essay*. However, due to the simplification of Chinese characters after the foundation of the People's Republic of China, some originally different characters such as "絜"(a synonymy of "洁") written by Zhou were replaced by the same simplified Chinese character. Consequently, there are more than 990 Chinese characters in the simplified Chinese version of *One-Thousand-Character Essay*.

第二课　金生丽水

Lesson Two　Gold from the Bottom of the Jinsha River

1. 描红并注音(Trace strokes and add pinyin)

( )

生

( )

水

( )

玉

( )

光

( )

果

( )

羽

2. 话题导入(Topic introduction)

说说你印象最深的五个中国汉字是什么。为什么？

What are the five Chinese characters that impress you most? And why?

Jīn	shēng	lì	shuǐ①	,	yù②	chū	kūn	gāng③	。
金	生	丽	水	，	玉	出	昆	冈	。
Jiàn	hào	jù	què④	,	zhū	chēng	yè	guāng⑤	。
剑	号	巨	阙	，	珠	称	夜	光	。
Guǒ	zhēn	lǐ	nài⑥	,	cài	zhòng	jiè	jiāng	。
果	珍	李	柰	，	菜	重	芥	姜	。
Hǎi	xián	hé	dàn	,	lín	qián	yǔ	xiáng	。
海	咸	河	淡	，	鳞	潜	羽	翔	。

1. 注释(Notes)

①丽水：即丽江，又名金沙江(Lijiang, also known as Jinsha River)。

②玉(jade)：一种矿物质。

③昆冈：昆仑山(Mount Kunlun)。

④巨阙：越王命令匠人欧冶子铸造了五把宝剑，巨阙是其中最锋利的一把(The King of Yue ordered the craftsman Ou Yezi to cast five swords, of which Juque was the sharpest)。

⑤夜光：《搜神记》中说，隋侯救了一条受伤的大蛇，后来大蛇带了一颗珍珠来报答他的恩情，那颗珍珠夜间放射出的光辉能照亮整个殿堂，人称"夜光珠"[*Sou Shen Ji* (*Stories of Immortals*)] said that Sui Hou rescued a wounded snake, and later the snake brought a pearl to repay his kindness. The brilliance of the pearl at night can illuminate the whole hall, known as the "luminous pearl")。

⑥柰：是中国的一种传统水果，比苹果小，果肉绵而不脆(a kind of fruit)。

2. 原文大意(Paraphrase)

金子从金沙江底产出，玉石来自昆仑山脉。

最有名的宝剑叫"巨阙"，最宝贵的珍珠叫"夜光"。

水果中最珍贵的是李子和柰，蔬菜中最重要的是芥和姜。

海水是咸的，河水是淡的；鱼儿在水中潜游，鸟儿在空中飞翔。

汉字学习 Chinese character

金	ノ 𠆢 𠆢 全 全 余 金 金										

拼音	jīn
词性	名词(n.)
释义	一种金属(a kind of metal);钱(money)
搭配	金属(metal);现金(cash)
例句	银是一种金属。Silver is a metal. 餐厅可以使用现金。Cash is accepted in the restaurant.

丽	一 丅 丆 厅 两 丽 丽										

拼音	lì
词性	形容词(adj.)
释义	美丽的(beautiful)
搭配	美丽(beautiful)
例句	这里的风景真美丽。The scenery is so beautiful here.

玉	一 二 干 王 玉										

拼音	yù
词性	名词(n.)
释义	石头的一种(a kind of stone)
搭配	碧玉(jasper)
例句	这块石头像碧玉一样。This stone is like jasper.

巨	一 𠃍 𠃍 巨 巨										

拼音	jù
词性	形容词(adj.)

释义	很大的(huge)
搭配	巨大(huge)
例句	那座山的下面,有个巨大的洞。 There is a huge hole under that mountain.

珠

拼音	zhū
词性	名词(n.)
释义	蚌壳内分泌物结成的有光小圆体(small shiny objects formed by secretions from a clam shell)
搭配	珍珠(pearl)
例句	那位女士戴着一条珍珠项链。The lady is wearing a pearl necklace.

称

拼音	chēng
词性	动词(v.)
释义	叫做(be known as);赞扬(praise)
搭配	称呼(address);称赞(praise)
例句	直接称呼老师的名字是不礼貌的。 It is rude to call your teacher by his name. 李老师称赞他进步很快。Mr. Li praised him for his rapid progress.

光

拼音	guāng
词性	名词(n.)
释义	明亮(light)
搭配	阳光(sunlight)
例句	春天的阳光很暖和。The spring sun is very warm.

珍

拼音	zhēn
词性	形容词(adj.)
释义	贵重的(precious)
搭配	珍贵(rare)
例句	博物馆收藏了大量珍贵的文物。 The museum has a large collection of precious cultural relics.

李

拼音	lǐ
词性	名词(n.)
释义	一种水果(a kind of fruit，plum)；出行带的物品(items to bring)
搭配	李子(plum)；行李箱(suitcase)
例句	你喜欢吃李子吗？Do you like eating plums? 李华经常带着这个行李箱出差。 Li Hua often takes this suitcase on business trips.

咸

拼音	xián
词性	形容词(adj.)
释义	含盐分多的(salty)
搭配	咸的(salty)
例句	这个菜是咸的。This dish is salty.

淡

拼音	dàn
词性	形容词(adj.)

释义	含盐分少的(less salty; not thick)
搭配	淡水(freshwater); 清淡(light)
例句	世界上最大的淡水湖是苏必利尔湖。 The largest freshwater lake in the world is Lake Superior. 这碗汤味道清淡。This soup has a light taste.

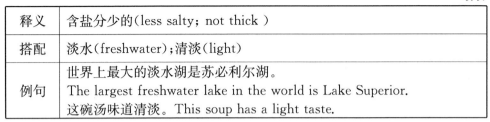

拼音	yǔ
词性	名词(n.)
释义	鸟的毛(a bird's feather)
搭配	羽毛(feather)
例句	那些小鸟的羽毛是棕色的。 The feathers of those young birds are brown.

四 日常对话 Dialogue

(一) 参观动物园 (Visiting the zoo)

李 华：今天天气很好，我们一起去参观动物园吧？

张丽丽：好啊，是个不错的想法！

李 华：你最喜欢的动物是什么？

张丽丽：我最喜欢的动物是小鸟。

李 华：为什么？

张丽丽：因为它们能够在天空中自由地飞翔。你最喜欢的动物是什么？

李 华：我最喜欢的动物是大熊猫。

张丽丽：走吧，我们一起去动物园寻找它们吧！

(二) 水源(Water sources)

李华：Nǐ zhī dao shì jiè shang shuǐ yǒu nǎ xiē zhǒng lèi ma
李　华：你知道世界上水有哪些种类吗？

张丽丽：Wǒ zhī dao　Shuǐ fēn wéi dàn shuǐ hé xián shuǐ
张　丽　丽：我知道。水分为淡水和咸水。

李华：Duì　Dàn shuǐ yì bān lái yuán yú hé liú hé hú pō　xián shuǐ yì bān
李　华：对。淡水一般来源于河流和湖泊，咸水一般
lái yuán yú hǎi yáng
来源于海洋。

张丽丽：Shén me lèi xíng de shuǐ dōu shì dì qiú shang bǎo guì de zī yuán
张　丽　丽：什么类型的水都是地球上宝贵的资源。

李华：Wǒ men yí dìng yào bǎo hù rén lèi lài yǐ shēng cún de shuǐ zī yuán
李　华：我们一定要保护人类赖以生存的水资源！

1. 连词：一边……一边

用法：连接两个同时发生的动作。

句型：主语＋一边＋动作1＋一边＋动作2。

例句：我们一边唱歌一边跳舞。

　　　李华一边听音乐一边走路。

2. 感叹句："真……啊！"和"太……了"

用法：表达说话者说话时的惊异、喜悦、愤怒、气愤等感情。

句型：真＋adj.＋啊！太＋adj.＋了！

例句：这花真漂亮啊！这花太漂亮了！

　　　他真高啊！他太高了！

六 课后练习 Exercises

1. 写一写(Writing)

根据拼音写汉字。

Write down the corresponding characters according to pinyin.

jīn _____ guāng _____ guǒ _____ dàn _____ yǔ _____

千字文

2. 填一填(Blank-filling)

用课文中的汉字填空。
Fill the following blanks with characters in the text.

(1) 多么美_____的花朵！
(2) 李老师_____赞他进步很快。
(3) 春天的阳_____很暖和。

3. 连一连(Matching)

把右列的汉字与左列的汉字相连组词。
Match characters in the right column with one in the left column to form a phrase.

金　　　　　　　　玉
碧　　　　　　　　淡
珠　　　　　　　　属
清　　　　　　　　宝

4. 默一默(Writing from memory)

根据课文内容填空。
Fill in the blanks according to the text.

金生_____水，_____出昆冈。
海咸_____淡，鳞潜_____翔。

5. 说一说(Talking)

根据所给场景，编写对话并练习。
Based on the given situations, make dialogues and practice.

说说你最喜欢的动物是什么？
示例：你最喜欢的动物是什么？
　　　我最喜欢的动物是大熊猫。你呢？

....

....

....

玉

　　"玉"是中国传统(chuán tǒng)文化中一个不可忽视(hū shì)的部分,中国人常用一句俗(sú)语"黄金有价玉无价"来表达玉的珍贵(zhēn guì)和价值(jià zhí)连城。在中国文化中,"玉"不仅珍贵,而且高洁。中国人常用"宁(nìng)为玉碎(yù suì),不为瓦全"来形容一个人的高尚(shàng)气节。随(suí)着社会的变化,"玉"也不再是贵族(guì zú)专属(shǔ),而渐渐(jiàn jiàn)走进了普通人家。

　　"Jade" is a part of Chinese traditional culture that cannot be ignored. Chinese people often uses a common saying "gold is valuable and jade is priceless" to express the preciousness and invaluableness of jade. In Chinese culture, "jade" is not only precious but also noble. Chinese people often describe a person's noble integrity by "better to die with honor than to survive in disgrace". With the changes in society, "jade" is no longer exclusive to nobles, but gradually enters ordinary people's homes.

第三课　龙师火帝

Lesson Three　Fuxi and Shennong

1. **描红并注音**(Trace strokes and add pinyin)

（　）
龙

（　）
火

（　）
鸟

（　）
文

（　）
字

（　）
衣

2. 话题导入(Topic introduction)

说说你知道古代中国有哪些皇帝吗?

Do you know emperors in early ancient China? Try to list some names.

学习原文 Text

Lóng	shī	huǒ	dì	niǎo	guān	rén	huáng
龙	师	火	帝	, 鸟	官	人	皇 。

Shǐ	zhì	wén	zì	nǎi	fú①	yī	shang
始	制	文	字	, 乃	服	衣	裳 。

Tuī②	wèi	ràng③	guó	Yǒu	Yú	Táo	Táng
推	位	让	国	, 有	虞	陶	唐 。

Diào④	mín	fá⑤	zuì⑥	Zhōu	Fā	Yīn	Tāng
吊	民	伐	罪	, 周	发	殷	汤 。

1. 注释(Notes)

①服:穿上(wear)。

②推:推辞(decline)。

③让:禅让(abdication)。

④吊:慰问,关心(mourn)。

⑤伐:讨伐(crusade against)。

⑥罪:有罪的统治者(a guilty ruler)。

2. 原文大意(Paraphrase)

伏羲氏、神农氏、少昊氏和人皇氏都是中国上古的皇帝、官员。

仓颉创造了文字,嫘祖制作了衣裳。

有虞和陶唐英明无私,禅让自己的王位。

周朝的姬发和殷朝的汤,他们慰问受苦的人民,讨伐专横的暴君。

汉字学习 Chinese character

龙	一	ナ	尢	龙	龙						
拼音	lóng										

词性	名词(n.)
释义	古代传说中一种神异动物(dragon)
搭配	水龙头(water tap)
例句	洗完手要记得关紧水龙头。 Remember to turn off the tap after washing your hands.

官

拼音	guān
词性	名词(n.)
释义	政府工作人员(official)
搭配	官方(official);官员(official)
例句	他是一名政府官员。 He is a government official.

始

拼音	shǐ
词性	名词(n.)
释义	最初(beginning)
搭配	始终(always)
例句	神经科医生始终严格遵守保密原则。 A shrink always strictly follows the principle of confidentiality.

制

拼音	zhì
词性	动词(v.)
释义	造;作(make)
搭配	制造(manufacture)

例句	制造木杆铅笔需要大量的木材。 Making wooden pencils needs a lot of wood.

拼音	mín
词性	名词(n.)
释义	人(person)；人群(people)
搭配	公民(citizen)
例句	公民有接受教育的权利。 Citizens are entitled to education.

拼音	tāng
词性	名词(n.)
释义	殷朝的皇帝(the emperor of the Yin Dynasty)；菜肴的一种(a type of dish)
搭配	米汤(the rice soup)
例句	大量的维生素都溶解在米汤里。 A lot of vitamins are dissolved in the rice soup.

四 日常对话 Dialogue

（一）下雨了 (Raining)

Lǐ Huá: Lì li, nǐ jīn tiān hái yǒu kè ma
李　华：丽丽，你今天还有课吗？

Zhāng Lì li: Wǒ jīn tiān de kè dōu shàng wán le
张丽丽：我今天的课都上完了。

Lǐ Huá: Tài hǎo le Wǒ men yì qǐ chū qù wán ba
李　华：太好了！我们一起出去玩吧。

Zhāng Lì li: Bù xíng wài miàn xià yǔ le
张丽丽：不行，外面下雨了。

Liú Fāng: Nǐ men zài shuō shén me ne
刘　芳：你们在说什么呢？

张丽丽:我们想出去玩,但是外面下雨了。

刘 芳:真可惜,你们下次再去吧。

(二)教室的灯亮着(The lights are on in the classroom)

刘 芳:这么晚了,教室的灯怎么还开着?

陈士杰:我去看看。

刘 芳:丽丽在里面复习汉语呢。

陈士杰:她这么晚还在看书,真爱学习。

刘 芳:既然灯开着,要不我们也去看书吧。

陈士杰:我还有点儿事情,就不去了。

刘 芳:好的。

五、语法知识 Grammar

1. 连词:但是

用法:用在后半句,表达转折,用在主语前,常与"虽然"等词语连用。

句型:虽然……,但是……。

例句:虽然天阴了,但是没有下雨。

　　　虽然他想去,但是妈妈不让。

　　　虽然他80岁了,但是身体很好。

2. 动态助词:着

用法:表示动作或者状态的持续,常用在动词后。

句型:动词+着。

例句:他穿着一件白衬衫。

　　　电风扇一直开着。

　　　我深深爱着他。

六 课后练习 Exercises

1. 写一写(Writing)

根据拼音写汉字。
Writing down the corresponding characters according to pinyin.

zhì _____造   mín 公_____   tāng 米_____

2. 连一连(Matching)

把右列的汉字与左列的汉字相连组词。
Match characters in the right column with one in the left column to form a phrase.

但   头
龙   是
始   方
人   终
官   群

3. 填一填(Blank-filling)

用本课学习的汉字填空。
Fill the following blanks with characters in the text.

(1) 他_____终记得离开教室要锁门。
(2) 公_____依法享有权利。
(3) 我饿了,我想喝米_____。
(4) 今天_____方发布了一条重要通知。

4. 默一默(Writing from memory)

根据课文内容填空。
Fill in the blanks according to the text.

_____师火帝,鸟官人皇。
_____ _____文字,乃服衣裳。
吊_____伐罪,周发殷_____。

5. 说一说(Talking)

根据提示,编写对话并练习。
Based on the given tips, make dialogues and practice.

说一说你最喜欢什么样的天气。为什么?

提示:晴天　阴天　下雨　下雪

我最喜欢……,因为……。

....
....
....

中国服饰

中国的服饰多种多样。除了一些特殊场合,现代中国人很少穿着传（chuán）统（tǒng）服饰,取而代之的是西式（shì）服饰。

中国的传统服饰被称为汉服,意为汉族（zú）人穿着的服装。汉服最初（chū）是根据《周礼》所创（chuàng）的。在后来的朝（cháo）代（dài）中,汉服又出现了其他样式（shì）,体现了汉族人对美（měi）的追（zhuī）求和向往（wǎng）。

随着人们对传统文化的关注升温,汉服也变得流（liú）行起来。汉服分为许（xǔ）多种类（lèi）,衣服的结构（gòu）和布（bù）料（liào）是区（qū）别不同款（kuǎn）式的汉服的标（biāo）准（zhǔn）。汉服有两种基（jī）本形式:上衣下裳（cháng）和衣裳连（lián）属（zhǔ）。

Chinese clothes are of various forms. Nowadays, except for some special occasions, Chinese people usually wear western-style clothes instead of traditional Chinese clothes.

Traditional Chinese clothes are called Hanfu, which means the clothes worn by the Han nationality group. Hanfu was originally created according to the *Rites of Zhou*. In the following dynasties, some other forms of Hanfu appeared, which shows the Han nationality's pursuit of aestheticism.

Nowadays, people have become more and more interested in traditional Chinese cultures. Consequently, Hanfu has also attracted more and more attention around the world. Hanfu can be generally classified into two categories according to their fabric and structure: two-piece Hanfu and one-piece Hanfu.

第四课　坐朝问道

Lesson Four　Governing a State

1. 描红并注音(Trace strokes and add pinyin)

( )
坐

( )
问

( )
爱

( )
化

( )
草

( )
万

2. 话题导入(Topic introduction)

谈谈你关于"天下和平"的观点。

Talk about your view of "the peace of world".

Zuò 坐	cháo 朝	wèn 问	dào① 道,	chuí 垂	gǒng② 拱	píng 平	zhāng③ 章。
Ài 爱	yù 育	lí 黎	shǒu④ 首,	chén 臣	fú 伏	róng 戎	qiāng⑤ 羌。
Xiá 遐	ěr⑥ 迩	yī 一	tǐ 体,	shuài 率	bīn⑦ 宾	guī 归	wáng 王。
Míng 鸣	fèng 凤	zài 在	zhú 竹,	bái 白	jū⑧ 驹	shí 食	chǎng 场。
Huà 化	bèi⑨ 被	cǎo 草	mù 木,	lài 赖	jí 及	wàn 万	fāng 方。

1. 注释(Notes)

①道:治理国家的方法(methods of governing the country)。

②拱:拱手(show respect by cupping one hand in the other before one's chest)。

③章:显现成绩(show the achievement)。

④黎首:老百姓,人民(civilian)。

⑤戎羌:各族人民(people of ethnic minorities)。

⑥遐迩:远近(far and near)。

⑦率宾:所有的人民(all the civilians)。

⑧驹:小马(pony)。

⑨被:覆盖(cover)。

2. 原文大意(Paraphrase)

国君坐在朝堂上,询问治国理政之道。

大臣垂衣拱手,思考治理之策;天下太平,彰显他们的功绩。

他们爱护人民,让各民族人民都臣服归顺。

全天下成为一个整体,所有老百姓都服从君主的统治。

凤凰在竹林中鸣叫,小白马在草场上吃草。

君主的贤德让草木都受到恩泽,君主的恩惠遍及天下百姓。

三 汉字学习 Chinese character

第四课 坐朝问道

朝

拼音	cháo
词性	名词(n.)
释义	厅堂(court)
搭配	朝代(dynasty)
例句	汉和唐,是历史上最能代表中国的两个朝代。 The Han and Tang dynasties are the two most representative dynasties of China in history.

章

拼音	zhāng
词性	动词(v.)
释义	同"彰",显露(show)
搭配	文章(article)
例句	王老师喜欢写文章。 Miss Wang likes writing articles.

首

拼音	shǒu
词性	名词(n.)
释义	头(head)
搭配	首先(first)
例句	我爱读的书首先是经典。 The books I like to read are classics first.

率

拼音	shuài
词性	动词(v.)
释义	带领(lead)
搭配	坦率(frank)
例句	做人需要诚实坦率。 People need to be honest and frank.

宾

拼音	bīn
词性	名词(n.)
释义	人(people)
搭配	宾馆(hotel)
例句	小明住在一家四星级豪华宾馆里。 Xiaoming lives in a luxurious four-star hotel.

归

拼音	guī
词性	动词(v.)
释义	返回(back)
搭配	归还(give back)
例句	借用的图书要按时归还。 Borrowed books must be returned on time.

化

拼音	huà
词性	名词(n.)
释义	教(education)

搭配	变化(change)
例句	计划往往赶不上变化。 Plans often fail to keep up with changes.

拼音	bèi
词性	动词(v.)
释义	覆盖(cover)
搭配	被子(quilt)
例句	晚上，妈妈给我悄悄地盖上被子。 At night, my mother quietly covers me with the quilt.

拼音	mù
词性	名词(n.)
释义	树(tree)
搭配	木头(wood)
例句	你用手无法从木头里拔出钉子。 You can't pull a nail out of the wood by hand.

拼音	jí
词性	动词(v.)
释义	达到(reach)
搭配	及格(pass)
例句	小明每年体育成绩都不及格。 Xiaoming fails PE every year.

四、日常对话 / Dialogue

（一）新生报到 (Freshmen Registration)

刘 芳：同学，你好，你是大一新生吗？

李 华：是的，我叫李华。今天来学校报到。

刘 芳：你是哪个学院的？

李 华：我是文学院的。你知道文学院在哪儿报到吗？

刘 芳：我也是文学院的，我带你过去报到吧。

李 华：好的，谢谢你。

（二）问路 (Ask for directions)

陈士杰：丽丽，你做了老师的作业了吗？

张丽丽：作业是写一篇文章吗？

陈士杰：是的，我不知道那篇文章怎么写。

张丽丽：你可以去图书馆查一些资料。

陈士杰：那你知道图书馆怎么走吗？

张丽丽：知道。你向前一直走就会看到，图书馆就在你的右边。

陈士杰：谢谢你，丽丽，再见。

张丽丽：再见。

五、语法知识 / Grammar

1. 疑问代词：哪

用法：询问地点。

句型:主语+动词+哪(儿)。
例句:你想要去哪儿?
　　　报到处在哪儿?

2. 介词:"向"和"在"

用法:表达路线。
句型:主语+向+方向词,名词+在+方向词。
例句:你向前直走,图书馆在你的右边。
　　　你向左跑,超市在你的左边。

1. 写一写(Writing)

根据拼音写汉字。

Write down the corresponding characters according to pinyin.

　shuài　　　　　　　bèi　　　　　　　huà
坦_____　　　　_____子　　　　变_____

2. 连一连(Matching)

把右列的汉字与左列的拼音相匹配。

Match a character in the right column with its correspondent pinyin in the left column.

平　　　　　　　　　　zhāng
迹　　　　　　　　　　huà
草　　　　　　　　　　píng
章　　　　　　　　　　ěr
化　　　　　　　　　　cǎo

3. 填一填(Blank-filling)

用课文中的汉字填空。

Fill the following blanks with characters in the text.

(1) 小李昨天住在一家豪华_____馆里。
(2) 从图书馆借图书要按时_____还。
(3) 小明今天语文考试_____格。
(4) 丽丽喜欢写文_____。

4. 默一默 (Writing from memory)

根据课文内容填空。
Fill in the blanks according to the text.

坐朝_____ _____,垂拱平章。

鸣凤在竹,_____ _____ _____场。

_____ _____ _____木,赖及万方。

5. 说一说 (Talking)

根据所给场景,编写对话并练习。
Based on the given situations, make dialogues and practice.

小丽刚搬家,她想要出去买一些生活用品,但是她迷路了,于是她找了一位热心的路人询问超市在哪儿。

提示:哪儿　向前一直走　在……左边(右边)

....

....

科举制度

科举制度是古代中国及受中国影响的日本、朝鲜、越南等国家选拔人才的考试制度。科举考试通常分为地方上的乡试、中央的省试(唐宋金元时期)或会试(明清时期)与殿试。科举制度扩展了国家引进人才的社会方式,吸收了大量出身于中下层的社会人士进入统治阶级。

The imperial civil service examination system was the fairest form of talent selection adopted in the feudal time in China as well as some neighboring countries like Japan, Korea and Vietnam. The imperial civil service examination was usually divided into local township examination, central provincial examination (Shengshi, during the Tang-song Period; or, Huishi, during the Ming-Qing Period) and palace examination. The imperial civil service examination system has expanded the social way of recruiting talents by the government and brought in a large number of people from middle and lower levels into the ruling class.

第五课　盖此身发

Lesson Five　Self-cultivation

一、课前练习 Warm-up

1. 描红并注音(Trace strokes and add pinyin)

2. 话题导入(Topic introduction)

你认为一个优秀的人应该具备哪些品质？

What qualities do you think an excellent person should have?

```
Gài    cǐ    shēn   fà        sì    dà①    wǔ    cháng②
盖     此    身     发    ，   四    大     五    常    。

Gōng   wéi   jū    yǎng③     qǐ    gǎn    huǐ   shāng
恭     惟    鞠    养    ，   岂    敢     毁    伤    。

Nǚ     mù    zhēn  jié       nán   xiào   cái   liáng
女     慕    贞    洁    ，   男    效     才    良    。

Zhī    guò   bì    gǎi       dé    néng   mò    wàng
知     过    必    改    ，   得    能     莫    忘    。

Wǎng④  tán   bǐ    duǎn      mǐ⑤   shì⑥   jǐ    cháng
罔     谈    彼    短    ，   靡    恃     己    长    。

Xìn    shǐ   kě    fù        qì    yù     nán   liáng
信     使    可    覆    ，   器    欲     难    量    。

Mò⑦    bēi   sī    rǎn       shī   zàn    gāo   yáng⑧
墨     悲    丝    染    ，   《诗》赞     羔    羊    。
```

1. 注释(Notes)

①四大:指地、水、风和火,古人认为万物皆源于这四大元素(four substances：earth, water, wind and fire, which, believed by ancient people, make up everything in the world.)。

②五常:封建社会中五种伦理道德:仁、义、礼、智、信(five ethics in the feudal society：benevolence, righteousness, courtesy, wisdom and faith)。

③鞠养:抚养、养育(bring up)。

④罔:无,没有(without)。

⑤靡:不要(do not)。

⑥恃:依仗,依靠(rely on)。

⑦墨:墨子,战国初期思想家,墨家学派创始人(Mozi, a thinker of the Warring States, founder of the Mo School)。

⑧羔羊:表示人的品质像羊毛一样纯净洁白(Human's qualities are as pure and white as wool)。

2. 原文大意(Paraphrase)

人们的身体发肤,关系到天地伦常。
虔诚地想着父母的抚养,哪里敢随便将身体损伤。
女子应该忠贞高洁,男子应当德才兼备。
如果知道自己有过错就一定要改正,坚持发挥自己的长处。
不要谈论别人的短处,也不要过分倚仗自己的长处。
诚实的品质才能经得起时间的考验,器量要大得让人难以估量。
墨子悲叹白丝被染上了杂色,《诗经》赞颂始终洁白的羔羊毛色。

汉字学习 Chinese character

盖											

拼音	gài
词性	名词(*n.*);动词(*v.*)
释义	用于器皿的遮蔽(lid of a vessel);遮住(cover)
搭配	覆盖,掩盖(cover on sth.);膝盖(knee)
例句	中国医保已经覆盖13.6亿人口。 China's health insurance already covers 1.36 billion people.

此											

拼音	cǐ
词性	代词(*pron.*)
释义	这,这个(this)
搭配	因此(therefore);彼此(each other)
例句	他想出国学习,因此参加了托福考试。 He wanted to study abroad, therefore, he took the TOEFL.

敢											

拼音	gǎn

续表

词性	动词(v.)
释义	不怕做某事(dare to do something)
搭配	勇敢(courageous);不敢当(feel flattered)
例句	她不敢去移动那些东西。 She didn't dare to move those things.

伤

拼音	shāng
词性	动词(v.)
释义	使损坏(break something)
搭配	令人伤心的(grievous);伤脑筋(bothersome)
例句	这消息真令人伤心。 This news is really grievous.

效

拼音	xiào
词性	名词(n.)
释义	效果(effect);影响(influence)
搭配	效果(effect);效率(efficiency)
例句	你越早去找医生,治疗效果会越好。 The sooner you go to the doctor, the better the treatment will be.

良

拼音	liáng
词性	形容词(adj.)
释义	好的(well, good)
搭配	良好(good);改良(improvement)

例句	良好的教学环境对于提高教学效果至关重要。 A good education environment is essential for effective teaching.

谈

拼音	tán
词性	动词(*v.*)
释义	与某人说话(talk to someone)
搭配	谈判(negotiation)
例句	两个国家正在进行谈判。 The two countries are negotiating.

彼

拼音	bǐ
词性	代词(*pron.*)
释义	那个(that)
搭配	彼此(each other)
例句	我们应该彼此互相帮助,互相学习。 We should help and learn from each other.

器

拼音	qì
词性	名词(*n.*)
释义	工具(tool)
搭配	充电器(charger);机器(machine)
例句	我是活生生的人,不是机器! I am a living human being, not a machine!

拼音	yáng
词性	名词(n.)
释义	一种食草动物(a herbivorous animal, sheep, goat)
搭配	羊肉(mutton)
例句	明天我要去吃羊肉。 I'm going to eat mutton tomorrow.

拼音	shī
词性	名词(n.)
释义	一种文体(a style of writing, poem)
搭配	诗人(poet);诗歌(poem)
例句	李白是中国古代最伟大的诗人之一。 Li Bai is one of the greatest poets of ancient China.

拼音	bēi
词性	形容词(adj.)
释义	伤心(feel sad)
搭配	悲观(pessimistic);悲观者(pessimist)
例句	悲观者通过心理训练可以转化成为乐观者。 A pessimist can be transformed into an optimist through psychological training.

拼音	zàn
词性	动词(v.)
释义	夸奖(praise);表扬(give credit for)
搭配	赞美,称赞(praise);赞成(agree)
例句	这个理论我不赞成。 I don't agree with this theory.

拼音	rǎn
词性	动词(v.)
释义	把东西放在颜料里使着色(put something in the paint to color it, dye);污染(contamination)
搭配	感染(infection)
例句	夏天气温高,易发生细菌感染。 In summer, bacterial infection is easy to occur.

四 日常对话 Dialogue

(一) 点外卖(Order take-out food)

李 华:刘芳,你要和我一起去食堂吃饭吗?

刘 芳:不去了,我打算在手机上点外卖。

李 华:你点了什么?

刘 芳:我点了汉堡和三个鸡翅。

李 华:这么多!你平常一两个汉堡就吃饱了。

刘芳：今天外卖有买一赠一的活动。

李华：真的吗？那我今天也点外卖。

（二）在图书馆(In the library)

李华：刘芳，你在看什么书？

刘芳：《三字经》，我已经认真地看过两遍了，很有趣。

李华：你经常在这里看书吗？

刘芳：对呀，图书馆很安静，大家都在看书，走路也很轻。

李华：那我们也要小声地说话，不要打扰别人。

刘芳：好的。等我看完这一页，我们就去外面聊天吧。

1. 概数

用法：相邻两个数词连用，表达一个大概的约数，如"一二（两）、七八"等。

句型：两个相邻的数字＋量词＋其他。

例句：我每天花一两个小时写作业。

这样的裙子她有七八条。

他大概三四十岁。

2. 结构助词：地

用法："地"前面的词修饰、限制后面的动作，表示某个动作怎么样。

句型：修饰、限制的词语＋地＋动词。

例句：她开心地笑了。

她悄悄地走了。

1. 写一写(Writing)

根据拼音写汉字。
Write down the corresponding characters according to pinyin.

rǎn	xiào	zàn	bēi	shī
污___	___率	___成	___观	___人

2. 连一连(Matching)

把右列的汉字与左列的汉字相连组词。
Match characters in the right column with one in the left column to form a phrase.

勇	此
彼	心
伤	染
感	敢
机	判
谈	器

3. 译一译(Translating)

用自己的话解释下列短语。
Explain the following phrases in your own words.

知过必改_____　　得能莫忘_____

罔谈彼短_____　　靡恃己长_____

4. 填一填(Blank-filling)

用合适的词完成下列表格。
Fill the following blanks with proper characters.

例:开心	地	笑
伤心	地	
轻轻	地	
	地	说
偷偷	地	
	地	跑

5. 说一说(Talking)

根据所给场景,编写对话并练习。
Based on the given situation, make dialogues and practice.

请谈一谈你最喜欢的食物,并说明原因。

提示:我最喜欢吃……,因为……

_____
_____

七 延伸学习 Extended reading

外　卖

人们常说"民以食为天",中国的饮食(yǐn shí)文化承载着民族(mín zú)文化,显示(xiǎn shì)着时代(shí dài)和习俗(xí sú)的变迁(biàn qiān)。随着(suí zhe)互联网(hù lián wǎng)深入我们生活(shēng huó)中的每一个角落(jiǎo luò),外卖逐渐成为(zhú jiàn chéng wéi)流行(liú xíng)的生活方式(shēng huó fāng shì)。只要指尖在手机上轻轻一点,选中喜欢的美食并付款(fù kuǎn),订单就会第一时间传递(chuán dì)到商家的手中。只要十几分钟,热气腾腾的可口(kě kǒu)美食就能被店家烹饪打包(pēng rèn dǎ bāo),并由快递员送到你的身边。外卖及时(jí shí)、方便、快捷的特点(tè diǎn)使得它一出现(chū xiàn),便受到(shòu dào)年轻人的欢迎,并作为(zuò wéi)一种生活方式被广泛接受(jiē shòu)。外卖作为一种新的餐饮文化,让传统(chuán tǒng)的饮食(yǐn shí)文化在新时代展现(zhǎn xiàn)出新的魅力(mèi lì)。

It is often said that "food is the soul of the people". Chinese food culture carries the national culture and shows the changes of times and customs. As the Internet penetrates into every corner of our life, takeout food online is becoming a popular way of life. When your fingertip lightly taps on the phone, selects the favorite food and pays, the order will be duly forwarded to the seller. In just more than ten minutes, a steaming, delicious meal can be packed up by restaurant staff and sent to you by a deliverer. Its timeliness, convenience and prompt delivery immediately attracted the attention of young people and has become their favorite. It has now been widely accepted as a way of life. As a new food culture, takeout makes the traditional food culture present a new image in the new era.

第六课　景行维贤

Lesson Six　Virtuous People and Philosophers

1. 描红并注音(Trace strokes and add pinyin)

( )
名

( )
表

( )
正

( )
谷

( )
因

( )
阴

2. 话题导入(Topic introduction)

你怎样理解帮助别人,自己也会获得快乐?请举例说明。

How do you understand "Helping others will make you happy"?

Jǐng xíng① wéi xián, kè② niàn zuò shèng。
景　行　维　贤　,　克　念　作　圣。

Dé jiàn míng lì, xíng duān biǎo zhèng。
德　建　名　立　,　形　端　表　正。

Kōng gǔ chuán shēng, xū táng xí③ tīng。
空　谷　传　声　,　虚　堂　习　听。

Huò yīn è jī, fú yuán shàn qìng④。
祸　因　恶　积　,　福　缘　善　庆。

Chǐ bì⑤ fēi bǎo, cùn yīn shì jìng⑥。
尺　璧　非　宝　,　寸　阴　是　竞。

1. 注释(Notes)

①景行:光明正大的行为(just and honorable act)。

②克:能,能够(able)。

③习:反复做(exercise repeatedly)。

④庆:回报(return)。

⑤璧:美玉的通称(jade in general)。

⑥竞:争取(strive for)。

2. 原文大意(Paraphrase)

向有贤德的品行的人看齐,克制私欲,效仿圣人。

有好的品德就会有好的名声,形体端庄,仪表就会正直。

空旷的山谷中声音会传得很远,宽敞的厅堂里可以听到清晰的说话声。

灾祸是恶行的积累,福气是善良的回报。

一尺长的美玉也并不可贵,而即使片刻的光阴也要争取。

汉字学习
Chinese character

景

拼音	jǐng
词性	名词(n.)
释义	高尚的(noble)
搭配	景色(scenery)
例句	夏威夷的景色非常美。 The scenery in Hawaii is very beautiful.

维

拼音	wéi
词性	动词(v.)
释义	系;连接(connect)
搭配	维护(maintain)
例句	我们应自觉维护校园的环境。 We should consciously maintain the campus' environment.

念

拼音	niàn
词性	名词(n.)
释义	想法(idea)
搭配	想念(miss)
例句	我时常想念过去美好的日子。 I often miss the good old days.

德

拼音	dé
词性	名词(n.)
释义	品行(moral standard)
搭配	品德(character)
例句	良好的社会教育有利于对孩子进行思想品德教育。 Good social education facilitates the education of children's moral character.

建

拼音	jiàn
词性	动词(v.)
释义	成立(establish)
搭配	建设(construct)
例句	文化建设对一个国家的发展非常重要。 Cultural construction is very important to the development of a country.

立

拼音	lì
词性	动词(v.)
释义	站(stand)
搭配	成立(set up)
例句	这家公司是2000年10月1日成立的。 This company was founded on 1 October 2000.

形									

拼音	xíng
词性	名词(*n.*)
释义	外在仪表(appearance)
搭配	形成(formation)
例句	青少年时期是形成正确价值观的重要时期。 Adolescence is an important stage for the formation of righteous values.

恶									

拼音	è
词性	形容词(*adj.*)
释义	不好,坏(bad)
搭配	恶劣(egregious)
例句	因为假期天气很恶劣,所以我们不能出去旅游。 We couldn't go out travelling because the weather was so bad during the holiday.

积									

拼音	jī
词性	动词(*v.*)
释义	聚集(assemble);从少到多(from less to more)
搭配	积累(accumulate)
例句	通过不断的练习,他积累了很多经验。 Through constant practice, he has accumulated a lot of experience.

福									

第六课 景行维贤

拼音	fú
词性	名词(n.)
释义	幸运(luck)
搭配	祝福(blessing)
例句	每个人都向他献上了祝福。 Everyone gave him a blessing.

善

拼音	shàn
词性	形容词(adj.)
释义	心地仁爱(love, kind)
搭配	善良(kind)
例句	王先生是一个善良的人。 Mr. Wang is a kind person.

庆

拼音	qìng
词性	动词(v.)
释义	回报(return);祝贺(celebrate)
搭配	庆祝(celebrate)
例句	大家聚在一起庆祝他的生日。 People got together to celebrate his birthday.

尺

拼音	chǐ
词性	量词(quantifier)

释义	长度单位(unit of length)
搭配	尺子(ruler)
例句	李明有三把尺子。Li Ming has three rulers.

宝

拼音	bǎo
词性	名词(n.)
释义	泛指珍贵的东西(generally refers to precious things)
搭配	宝贝(treasure)
例句	儿女都是父母的宝贝。 Children are the treasure of their parents.

寸

拼音	cùn
词性	量词(quantifier)
释义	长度单位(unit of length)
搭配	英寸(inch)
例句	一英寸约等于2.5厘米。 One inch is about 2.5 centimeters.

竞

拼音	jìng
词性	动词(v.)
释义	争取(strive for)
搭配	竞争(compete, competition)
例句	良性的竞争会促使我们进步。 Good competition will drive us forward.

四 日常对话 Dialogue

（一）网购 (Online shopping)

李华：网购真是方便极了！

刘芳：你在网上买了什么？

李华：我已经买了一条裤子，我还想再买一件衬衣。

刘芳：你觉得衣服的质量怎么样？

李华：我觉得比商场里的质量更好，而且价格更加便宜，我非常满意！

刘芳：因为有了这些软件，我们的生活更加方便。

（二）减肥 (Weight-losing)

李华：我最近胖了，我想减肥，你有什么好的建议吗？

刘芳：你可以通过运动来减肥。

李华：我已经尝试过运动了，很难坚持下去。

刘芳：那你可以多吃蔬菜。

李华：可是我最喜欢品尝美食了。

刘芳：那你可以在网上查找更多好的方法。

李华：好吧。

五 语法知识 Grammar

1. 感叹句：极；多

用法："极"常用在形容词后，"多"常用在形容词前，表示说话者强烈的情感。

句型:主语+形容词+极了;主语+多/多么+形容词!
例句:这个孩子可爱极了!
　　　这个经验多么重要!

2. 时间副词:已经

用法:表示时间已过,动作、事情或状况在某时间之前完成或出现。
句型:人/物+已经+动词+事情+了。
　　　人/物+已经+动词+了+事情。
例句:他已经到学校了。
　　　我们已经完成了公司的任务。

1. 写一写(Writing)

根据拼音写汉字。
Write down the corresponding characters according to pinyin.

jǐng	xíng	wéi	niàn	jī
___色	___成	___护	想___	___累

2. 连一连(Matching)

把右列的汉字与左列的汉字相连组词。
Match characters in the right column with one in the left column to form a phrase.

品　　　　　　　　　贝
建　　　　　　　　　劣
成　　　　　　　　　设
善　　　　　　　　　德
恶　　　　　　　　　立
庆　　　　　　　　　祝
宝　　　　　　　　　良

3. 填一填(Blank-filling)

用适当的汉字填空。
Fill the following blanks with proper characters.
(1) 海边的___色非常美。

(2) 我很想_____爷爷。

(3) 因为今天天气很_____劣，所以我没有外出。

(4) 李明有一颗_____良的心。

4. 默一默(Writing from memory)

根据课文内容填空。

Fill in the blanks according to the text.

(1) 祸因_____积

(2) _____缘_____庆

(3) _____璧非_____

(4) _____阴是_____

5. 说一说(Talking)

根据所给场景，编写对话并练习。

Based on the given situations, make dialogues and practice.

你朋友的身上有没有值得你学习的地方？请举例说明。

中国的 福 文 化
（fú wén huà）

福文化是中国传统的民俗文化，随着时代变迁而历久弥新，已经渗透到人们的日常生活之中，体现着中国人的生活观念和价值观，在每个人的身上都留下了印记。所谓的"福"，在过去指的是"福气""福运"，认为人们如果行善积德就会得到上天的帮助，平安顺利。人们会在过年时贴福字、做福包祈求福运的到来。而现在，人们认为福是"幸福"，寓意精神层面的满足。无论过去还是现在，人们对"福"字都十分喜爱，都寄托着对美好生活的向往与祝愿。

As a traditional Chinese folk culture, the Fu(福, fú, happiness) culture has been constantly updated with the changes of times. It has penetrated into people's daily life and embodied Chinese life concepts and values, leaving a mark on everyone. The so-called "Fu" in the past meant blessing and good luck. It was believed that if people did good deeds and accumulated virtues, they would get help from gods and be safe and successful. People will paste the Chinese character Fu on the New Year Day and make lucky bags to pray for good luck. Now, people think of Fu as happiness, indicating spiritual satisfaction. Whether in the past or at present, people are very fond of Fu, which expresses their yearning and wishes for a better life.

第七课　资父事君

Lesson Seven　Waiting on Your Father and Serving Your King

1. 描红并注音(Trace strokes and add pinyin)

( )
父

( )
孝

( )
力

( )
川

( )
不

( )
取

2. 话题导入(Topic introduction)

你认为我们应该怎样孝敬父母？

How to perform our filial duty to our parents?

一、学习原文 Text

资①父 事②君，曰 严③与 敬。
Zī fù shì jūn, yuē yán yǔ jìng.

孝 当 竭④力，忠 则 尽 命。
Xiào dāng jié lì, zhōng zé jìn mìng.

临 深 履 薄，夙 兴⑤温⑥清⑦。
Lín shēn lǚ bó, sù xīng wēn qìng.

似 兰 斯 馨，如 松 之 盛。
Sì lán sī xīn, rú sōng zhī shèng.

川 流 不 息，渊 澄⑧取 映。
Chuān liú bù xī, yuān chéng qǔ yìng.

1. 注释(Notes)

①资：奉养(support)。

②事：侍奉(serve)。

③严：认真(serious)。

④竭：用尽(exhaust)。

⑤夙兴：早起(rise early)。

⑥温：使……温暖(make…warm)。

⑦清：使……凉爽(make…cool)。

⑧澄：清澈干净(clear and clean)。

2. 原文大意(Paraphrase)

奉养父亲，侍奉君主，要严肃恭敬。

孝顺父母应该尽心尽力，忠于君主要不怕牺牲。

要像走在很深的山谷边、很薄的冰上那样谨慎小心，要早起晚睡，让父母感到冬天的温暖和夏天的凉爽。

让自己的德行像兰草那样清香，像松柏那样茂盛。

还能延及子孙，像大河川流不息；影响世人，像干净的水潭清澈照人。

资

拼音	zī
词性	动词(v.);名词(n.)
释义	供给(supply);钱财(money)
搭配	工资(salary);资金(capital)
例句	他的月工资是3000块。 His monthly salary is 3000 *yuan*.

父

拼音	fù
词性	名词(n.)
释义	爸爸(father)
搭配	父亲(father);父爱(fatherly love)
例句	我的父亲很帅。My father is a handsome guy.

严

拼音	yán
词性	形容词(adj.)
释义	不放松,认真(serious)
搭配	严格(strict);严肃(serious)
例句	他对待工作非常严格。He is very strict with his work.

与

拼音	yǔ

词性	介词(prep.)
释义	和(and)
搭配	参与(take part in)
例句	他参与了这项活动。He took part in this activity.

敬

拼音	jìng
词性	动词(v.)
释义	尊重(respect)
搭配	尊敬(respect);敬爱(admire)
例句	他尊敬每一位老师。 He respects every teacher.

当

拼音	dāng
词性	介词(prep.)
释义	组成时间短语,表示事件发生的时间(when)
搭配	当时(then);当面(in one's presence)
例句	当时丢钱的地方你还记得吗? Do you remember the place where you lost the money at that time?

尽

拼音	jìn
词性	动词(v.)
释义	完毕(finish);没有(without)

搭配	竭尽全力(do one's utmost)
例句	为了成功,大家都竭尽全力了。 In order to succeed, everyone had done their utmost.

命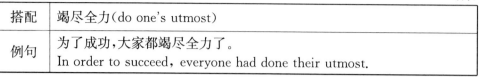

拼音	mìng
词性	名词(n.);动词(v.)
释义	注定的人生(destiny);指派(appoint)
搭配	命运(fate);命令(order);任命(appoint)
例句	他被任命为公司经理。 He was appointed manager of the company.

临

拼音	lín
词性	动词(v.)
释义	面对(face);靠近(near)
搭配	面临(face)
例句	面临问题时要冷静。Be calm when you are facing a problem.

深

拼音	shēn
词性	形容词(adj.)
释义	从上到下的距离(deep)
搭配	深度(depth);深沉(profound)
例句	测量海洋的深度非常困难。 It's very difficult to measure the depth of the ocean.

薄

拼音	bó
词性	形容词(*adj.*)
释义	厚度小(thin)
搭配	薄弱(weakness)；薄冰(thin ice)
例句	河面上结了一层薄冰。A thin layer of ice formed on the river.

似

拼音	sì
词性	副词(*adv.*)
释义	好像(like)；如同(as)
搭配	似乎(seem)；类似(similar)
例句	他似乎有点不开心。He seemed a little unhappy.

松

拼音	sōng
词性	名词(*n.*)
释义	一种常绿乔木(an evergreen tree, pine)
搭配	放松(relaxed)；轻松(easy)
例句	考大学对我来说是件轻松的事。Getting into college was easy for me.

之

拼音	zhī
词性	助词(*aux.*)

第七课 资父事君

释义	的(of)
搭配	总之(in a word)
例句	总之，我们要互相尊重。 In a word, we should respect each other.

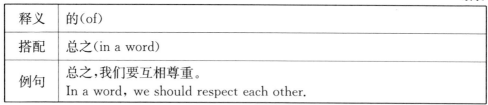

拼音	yìng
词性	动词(v.)
释义	照射(shine)；反映(reflect)
搭配	反射(reflect)
例句	标题反映了你要写的内容。 The title reflects what you are going to write about.

四 日常对话 Dialogue

（一）厘米和米(Centimeter and meter)

Lǐ Huá: Nǐ zhī dao lí mǐ hé mǐ ma
李　　华：你 知 道 厘 米 和 米 吗？

Zhāng Lì li: Zhī dao, lí mǐ hé mǐ dōu shì cháng dù dān wèi
张　丽 丽：知 道，厘 米 和 米 都 是 长 度 单 位。

Lǐ Huá: Shì de. Nà nǐ de shēn gāo shì duō shǎo
李　　华：是 的。那 你 的 身 高 是 多 少？

Zhāng Lì li: Wǒ de shēn gāo shì　　　lí mǐ
张　丽 丽：我 的 身 高 是 160 厘 米。

Lǐ Huá: Nà yòng mǐ biǎo shì ne
李　　华：那 用 米 表 示 呢？

Zhāng Lì li: Wǒ de shēng āo shì yī mǐ liù
张　丽 丽：我 的 身 高 是 一 米 六。

Lǐ Huá: Suǒ yǐ mǐ děng yú lí mǐ
李　　华：所 以 1 米 等 于 100 厘 米。

Zhāng Lì li: duì de nǐ hěn cōng ming
张　丽 丽：对 的，你 很 聪 明。

（二）倍数的表达（Expression of multiples）

刘　　芳：最近我在锻炼身体，吃得比较多了。

陈士杰：比以前多多少？

刘　　芳：我吃的是以前的两倍。

陈士杰：什么是两倍？

刘　　芳：比如我以前中午吃一碗饭，现在我吃两碗饭。2是1的两倍。

陈士杰：好的，我明白了。

1. 长度单位：厘米与米

用法：长度的度量单位，1米＝100厘米。

例句：三岁的宝宝大约一米高。

　　　虽然这个小辣椒只有三厘米长，但是真的很辣。

2. 数词：倍数的表达

用法：表示数目的增加，不能用于数目的减少。

例句：4是2的两倍。

　　　今年全家的收入是去年的1.5倍。

1. 写一写（Writing）

根据拼音写汉字。

Write down the corresponding characters according to pinyin.

　　　zī　　　　　　　mìng　　　　　　　fù
工＿＿＿　　　＿＿＿令　　　＿＿＿爱

2. 连一连(Matching)

把右列的汉字与左列的汉字相连组词。

Match characters in the right column with one in the left column to form a phrase.

严		取
深		奥
放		格
获		金
资		松

3. 填一填(Blank-filling)

用适当的汉字填空。

Fill the following blanks with proper characters.

(1) 我的数学老师比较_____格。

(2) 她将所有的_____金用于购买设备。

(3) 重在参与,你已经_____力了。

(4) 这次考试你不用太紧张,放_____就好。

4. 默一默(Writing from memory)

根据课文内容填空。

Fill in the blanks according to the text.

_____ _____事君,曰_____ _____敬。

孝_____竭_____,忠则_____ _____。

临_____履薄,夙兴_____ _____。

似兰斯馨,_____ _____ _____盛。

川流不息,渊澄_____ _____。

5. 说一说(Talking)

根据所给场景,编写对话并练习。

Based on the given situations, make dialogues and practice.

用长度单位来描述生活中出现的物品。

提示:厘米和米

"岁寒三友"

松有其独特(dú tè)的内涵,人们常以松(sōng)象征坚贞(jiān zhēn)。松枝高傲并且四季都是绿色的。《论语》夸它:岁寒,然后知松柏之后凋(diāo)也。文艺作品中,经常用松象征坚贞不屈的英雄气节。松与竹、梅一起,一直有着"岁寒三友"的美名,它们在寒冬里仍能保持绿色。松树象征常青不老,竹子象征君子品质,梅花象征冰清玉洁。

The pine, having its unique connotation, is often used by people to symbolize faithfulness. The pine branches are lofty and evergreen throughout the year. As it is praised in *The Confucian Analects*: Only in cold winter does one know that the pine and the cypress are the last to shed their leaves. In literary and artistic works, the pine is often adopted to represent the unyielding heroism. The pine tree, bamboo and plum blossom have always been known as "three cold-weather friends" for their evergreeness in cold winter. The pine tree symbolizes immortality; the bamboo the quality of the gentleman; and the plum blossom purity.

第八课　容止若思

Lesson Eight　Be Self-collected and Behave Prudently

1. 描红并注音(Trace strokes and add pinyin)

( )
止　丨 ト 卜 止

( )
言　丶 亠 䒑 言 言 言 言

( )
安　丶 宀 宀 安 安 安

( )
学　丶 丷 丷 丷 学 学 学

( )
甘　一 十 廿 甘 甘

( )
去　一 十 去 去 去

2. 话题导入(Topic introduction)

你最想从事的职业。为什么？

Your most desired occupation. And why?

第八课 容止若思

Róng	zhǐ	ruò	sī	yán	cí	ān	dìng
容	止	若	思	，言	辞	安	定 。
Dǔ①	chū	chéng	měi	shèn	zhōng	yí	lìng②
笃	初	诚	美	，慎	终	宜	令 。
Róng	yè	suǒ	jī	jí③	shèn	wú	jìng④
荣	业	所	基	，籍	甚	无	竟 。
Xué	yōu⑤	dēng	shì	shè⑥	zhí	cóng	zhèng
学	优	登	仕	，摄	职	从	政 。
Cún	yǐ	gān	táng⑦	qù	ér	yì	yǒng
存	以	甘	棠	，去	而	益	咏 。

1. 注释(Notes)

①笃：重视(attach importance to)；专注(concentrate on)。

②令：美好(good)。

③籍：作衬垫的东西,引申为凭借(rely on)。

④竟：同"境",边境(border)。

⑤学优：出自《论语》"学而优则仕"(Learning excellently is to become an official)之语。

⑥摄：代理(act as an agent)。

⑦甘棠：召公南巡时,为了不打扰民众,曾在一棵高大的甘棠树下判案办公；召公去世后,后人因怀念其德,一直不忍心砍伐掉那棵甘棠树,并作诗缅怀召公(During his inspection in the south, to avoid disturbing the people, Shaogong handled official business under a Gantang tree. After his death, people missed him, refused to cut down the Gantang tree and wrote poems commemorating Shaogong)。

2. 原文大意(Paraphrase)

仪容举止要沉静安详,言语措辞要稳重从容。

无论修身、求学,重视开头固然不错；认真去做,有好的结果更为重要。

这是一生荣誉的事业的基础,有此根基,发展就没有止境。

书读好了就能做官,可以担任职务,参与国政。

做官要像召公,周人为召公留下甘棠树,一直舍不得砍伐,对他倍加怀念。

三 汉字学习 / Chinese character

容

拼音	róng
词性	名词(n.)
释义	相貌(appearance);包含(include)
搭配	内容(content)
例句	这本书的主要内容是成语故事。 The main content of this book is stories about idiomatic expressions.

止

拼音	zhǐ
词性	名词(n.)
释义	行为(behavior);停住不动(stand still)
搭配	停止(stop)
例句	这次考试的报名已经停止了。 Registration for this exam has been closed.

辞

拼音	cí
词性	名词(n.);动词(v.)
释义	言语,说的话(speech);告别(farewell)
搭配	致辞(deliver a speech);辞职(resign)
例句	校长正在致辞。The principal is delivering a speech. 因为工作很辛苦,所以他决定辞职。 Because of the hard work, he decided to resign.

初

拼音	chū
词性	名词(n.)
释义	开始时,开始的部分(at the beginning)
搭配	最初(the first time)
例句	他最初来镇江,一点儿都不习惯。 He was not used to it when he first came to Zhenjiang.

诚

拼音	chéng
词性	副词(adv.);形容词(adj.)
释义	实在,的确(indeed);真心的(sincere)
搭配	诚实(honest)
例句	我相信他是诚实的。I believe he is honest.

美

拼音	měi
词性	形容词(adj.)
释义	好,善(well, good)
搭配	完美(perfect)
例句	没有人是完美的。Nobody is perfect.

终

拼音	zhōng
词性	名词(n.)
释义	尽头(end)

搭配	终点(destination)
例句	我们这次旅行的终点是镇江。The destination of our trip is Zhenjiang.

令 丿 人 𠆢 今 令

拼音	lìng
词性	名词(n.)
释义	上级对下级的指示(instructions from superiors to subordinates)
搭配	命令(command)
例句	士兵要服从上级命令。 The soldiers must obey the orders of their superiors.

荣 一 十 卄 芇 艼 荠 荠 荣

拼音	róng
词性	名词(n.)
释义	受人敬重(respected by others)
搭配	荣誉(honor)
例句	我们班获得歌唱比赛第一名,这是所有人的荣誉。 Our class won the first place in the singing competition, which is the honor of everyone.

基 一 十 卄 廿 甘 甘 其 其 其 基 基

拼音	jī
词性	名词(n.)
释义	建筑物的根脚(roots of buildings);最低层(the lowest level)
搭配	基础(base);基础的(basic)
例句	基础知识很重要。Basic knowledge is essential.

籍

拼音	jí
词性	名词(n.)
释义	隶属关系(affiliation)
搭配	国籍(nationality)
例句	你是什么国籍？What is your nationality?

甚

拼音	shèn
词性	副词(adv.)
释义	非常,极(very)
搭配	甚至(even)
例句	李华一整天都在学习,甚至忘记了吃饭。 Li Hua has been studying all day and even forgot to eat.

无

拼音	wú
词性	动词(v.)
释义	没有(without, do/does not have)
搭配	无聊(bored)
例句	没有事做,他觉得很无聊。He was bored with nothing to do.

登

第八课 容止若思

拼音	dēng
词性	动词(v.)
释义	上、升(rise)
搭配	登记(register)
例句	请登记个人信息。Please register your personal information.

拼音	shè
词性	动词(v.)
释义	拿(take);代理(act as an agent)
搭配	摄影(photography)
例句	我的一个朋友特别喜欢摄影。 One of my friends really likes photography.

拼音	zhí
词性	名词(n.)
释义	分内应做的事(duty)
搭配	职业(occupation)
例句	我们都希望有一份好职业。We all want a good job.

拼音	zhèng
词性	名词(n.)
释义	国家事务(state affairs)

搭配	政治(politics)
例句	教育能为政治培养人才。Education can nurture talents for politics.

拼音	cún
词性	动词(v.)
释义	保留,留下(keep)
搭配	保存(preserve)
例句	这些书保存得很好。These books are well preserved.

拼音	yì
词性	副词(adv.);形容词(adj.)
释义	更加(more);对……有好处(be beneficial to)
搭配	日益(increasingly);利益(benefit, interest)
例句	我的家乡日益美丽。My hometown is becoming increasingly beautiful. 我们不能做损害国家利益的事情。We cannot do things that harm the national interests.

四 日常对话 Dialogue

(一) 周末有什么安排吗? (Arrangements for the weekend)

Lǐ Huá: Nǐ zhè ge zhōu mò yǒu shén me ān pái ma
李 华:你这个周末有什么安排吗?

Zhāng Lì li: Wǒ zhǔn bèi qù tú shū guǎn xué xí
张 丽丽:我准备去图书馆学习。

Lǐ Huá: Nǐ qù tú shū guǎn kàn shū duì ma
李 华:你去图书馆看书,对吗?

Zhāng Lì li: Bú shì wǒ qù tú shū guǎn xiě qī mò zuò yè
张 丽丽:不是,我去图书馆写期末作业。

李　　华：好的，我这个周末去郊外野餐。

张　丽丽：祝你玩得开心。

(二) 去参观展览会 (Visiting the fair)

刘　　芳：明天下午学校有展览会，你去吗？

陈　士杰：我还不知道有展览会，你知道有什么活动吗？

刘　　芳：有各种美食，各类工艺品，还有服装走秀。

陈　士杰：哇，好棒，我也去。

刘　　芳：但是我听说活动要求参观者提前预约。

陈　士杰：那我们快去预约吧。

刘　　芳：好的。

1. 疑问词（吗）

用法：是非疑问句——用陈述句提出自己的意见、估计、要求等，然后用"好吗、行吗、成吗、可以吗"等征询对方的意见。

句型：陈述句，……吗？

例句：好吗：我们一起去，好吗？

　　　对吗：您要两张票，对吗？

　　　可以吗：中午吃面条，可以吗？

2. 代词（各，各位）

用法：**各**表示每个，彼此不同；**各位**表示每个人。

句型：各＋(量词)＋人/物；各位＋人。

例句：各人有各人的独特之处，不必模仿他人。

　　　各位请坐好，我们的电影马上就要开始了。

六 课后练习 Exercises

1. 写一写(Writing)

根据拼音写汉字。
Write down the corresponding characters according to pinyin.

ān	dìng	chéng	yán
____心	心神不____	____实	____行

2. 连一连(Matching)

把右列的汉字与左列的汉字相连组词。
Match characters in the right column with one in the left column to form a phrase.

甚　　　　　　　　聊
无　　　　　　　　存
保　　　　　　　　业
优　　　　　　　　容
内　　　　　　　　美
职　　　　　　　　至

3. 填一填(Blank-filling)

用适当的汉字填空。
Fill the following blanks with proper characters.

(1) 他向老板提出了_____职。

(2) 她的妈妈非常_____丽和优雅。

(3) 我有一个朋友特别喜欢_____影。

(4) 我们这次旅行的_____点是镇江。

(5) 李华一整天都在学习，_____至忘记了吃饭。

4. 默一默(Writing from memory)

根据课文内容填空。
Fill in the blanks according to the text.

____ ____若思，____辞____ ____。

笃初____ ____，慎____宜令。

荣____所____，籍____ ____ ____。

千字文

学_____登仕,摄_____从政。

存_____甘棠,去_____益咏。

5. 说一说(Talking)

根据所给场景,编写对话并练习。
Based on the given situations, make dialogues and practice.
询问自己的同学这周末的安排。
示例:你这个周末有什么安排吗?
　　　我周末打算去操场踢足球。

....

....

七 延伸学习 Extended reading

学而优则仕 (yōu zé shì)

"学而优则仕"这句话出自《论语》:"仕而优则学,学而优则仕。"

常(cháng)人只重"学而优则仕"这后半句,并以此激励(jī lì)自己刻苦(kè kǔ)读书,希望有一天能出人头地(chū rén tóu dì)。为政者则要看重前半句,善于(shàn yú)学习和思考,不断(bú duàn)提高自己、充实(chōng shí)自己,增强为人民服务的本领。

所以,这句话告诉我们人的一生是学习的一生,清楚自己的人生(rén shēng)方向,终身(zhōng shēn)学习,自我提升,无论何时、无论何地,不放过任何学习的机会。

This sentence comes from *The Confucian Analects*: "An official who performs his duty well should further his study and a scholar who is well-learned should be a government official to serve his fellow people."

Ordinary people only pay attention to the second half of "study and be an official", and use this to motivate themselves to study hard, hoping to stand out above others. Politicians should pay attention to the first half of the sentence, be good at learning and thinking, constantly improve and enrich themselves, and cultivate their ability to serve the people.

Therefore, this sentence tells us that "to live is to learn". We should have a clear picture of our life direction, devote ourselves to lifelong learning, and keep on improving ourselves. Wherever or whenever, never miss any opportunities to learn.

第九课　乐殊贵贱

Lesson Nine　Different Music for Different People

1. 描红(Trace strokes and add pinyin)

( )
上

( )
下

( )
夫

( )
母

( )
比

( )
交

2. 话题导入(Topic introduction)

说一说你和你的兄弟姐妹是怎么相处的?
How do you get along with your brothers and sisters?

乐^{yuè} 殊^{shū}① 贵^{guì} 贱^{jiàn}，礼^{lǐ} 别^{bié}② 尊^{zūn} 卑^{bēi}。
上^{Shàng} 和^{hé} 下^{xià} 睦^{mù}③，夫^{fū} 唱^{chàng} 妇^{fù} 随^{suí}④。
外^{Wài} 受^{shòu} 傅^{fù} 训^{xùn}，入^{rù} 奉^{fèng} 母^{mǔ} 仪^{yí}。
诸^{Zhū} 姑^{gū} 伯^{bó} 叔^{shū}，犹^{yóu}⑤ 子^{zǐ} 比^{bǐ} 儿^{ér}。
孔^{Kǒng} 怀^{huái}⑥ 兄^{xiōng} 弟^{dì}，同^{tóng} 气^{qì} 连^{lián} 枝^{zhī}。
交^{Jiāo} 友^{yǒu} 投^{tóu} 分^{fèn}，切^{qiē} 磨^{mó}⑦ 箴^{zhēn}⑧ 规^{guī}。

1. 注释(Notes)

①殊:不同(different)。

②别:区别(different)。

③睦:和睦(harmony)。

④随:跟随(follow)。

⑤犹:像(resemble)。

⑥孔怀:很思念(miss very much),后指兄弟之情。

⑦切磨:本指加工玉石等器物,此处引申为探究学问(Originally referring to the processing of jade and other artifacts; in this context, it refers to academic research)。

⑧箴(zhēn):劝诫、劝勉(exhort)。

2. 原文大意(Paraphrase)

音乐因人的身份贵贱而有不同,礼节根据人的地位高低而有区别。

上下要和睦相处,夫妇要一唱一随,协调和谐。

在外接受师傅的教导,在家遵从父母的教导。

对待姑姑、伯伯、叔叔等长辈,要像是他们的亲生子女一样。

兄弟之间要相互关心,因为一起承受父母亲情,如同树枝相连。

结交朋友要心意相合,要能学习上沟通交流,互相改进,品行上相互劝勉。

拼音	zūn
词性	形容词(adj.)
释义	高贵(noble)
搭配	尊敬(respect);尊重(revere)
例句	人们应该互相尊敬。 People should respect each other.

拼音	fū
词性	名词(n.)
释义	女子的配偶(woman's spouse)
搭配	丈夫(husband);夫妇(couple)
例句	她的丈夫是医生。Her husband is a doctor.

拼音	fù
词性	名词(n.)
释义	已婚的女子(married woman)
搭配	妇女(woman);夫妇(couple)
例句	她是一个已婚妇女。She is a married woman.

拼音	xùn
词性	动词(v.)
释义	教导(teach)
搭配	教训(lessons); 培训(training)
例句	这份工作要经过培训才能上岗。 This job requires training before being employed.

拼音	fù
词性	名词(n.)
释义	老师(teacher)
搭配	师傅(master)
例句	请师傅说具体一些。 Please tell me more specifics, master.

拼音	mǔ
词性	名词(n.)
释义	妈妈(mom)
搭配	母亲(mother)
例句	她是一位心地善良的母亲。 She is a kind-hearted mother.

拼音	fèng

词性	动词(v.)
释义	供养(support);伺候(wait on)
搭配	奉献(sacrifice)
例句	他很乐于奉献自己帮助别人。 He is happy to sacrifice himself to help others.

姑

拼音	gū
词性	名词(n.)
释义	父亲的姐妹(father's sister)
搭配	姑姑,姑妈(paternal aunt)
例句	我的姑姑特别漂亮。 My aunt is very beautiful.

叔

拼音	shū
词性	名词(n.)
释义	爸爸的兄弟(father's brother)
搭配	叔叔(paternal uncle)
例句	我的叔叔已经三十七岁了。 My uncle is already thirty-seven years old.

犹

拼音	yóu
词性	副词(adv.)
释义	好像(like);如同(as)
搭配	犹如(as if, like)
例句	平静的湖面犹如一面镜子。The calm lake is like a mirror.

怀

拼音	huái
词性	动词(v.)
释义	思念(miss)
搭配	怀念(miss)
例句	他总是很怀念他去世的妻子。 He always misses his departed wife.

连

拼音	lián
词性	动词(v.)
释义	相接(meet)
搭配	接连(in succession)
例句	他们家最近接连发生了几件奇怪的事。 Several strange things have happened to their family recently.

兄

拼音	xiōng
词性	名词(n.)
释义	哥哥(elder brother)
搭配	兄弟(brother)；兄长(elder brother)
例句	他是我的好兄弟。He is my good brother.

切

拼音	qiē
词性	动词(v.)
释义	交流,沟通(communicate)；吸取长处(learn from strengths)

搭配	亲切(kind)
例句	他是一位亲切温和的教授。 He is a kind and gentle professor.

投

拼音	tóu
词性	动词(v.)
释义	相合(agree with)
搭配	投篮(shoot)
例句	他投篮不太好。He doesn't shoot very well.

规

拼音	guī
词性	动词(v.)
释义	劝勉(urge)
搭配	规定(regulation)
例句	学生应该遵守学校的规定。 Students are expected to abide by the school's rules.

四 日常对话 Dialogue

(一) 午饭吃什么(What to have for lunch)

李　华：我们今天中午吃什么？

张丽丽：我想吃面条，面条里面放牛肉或者鸡蛋。

李　华：那我们一会儿就去吃吧，你要吃牛肉面还是鸡蛋面？

张丽丽：我都可以，鸡蛋面吧。你呢？

李　　华:我吃牛肉面。

张　丽　丽:那我们走吧。

(二) 假期去哪里(Where to spend the holiday)

刘　　芳:你这次假期想去哪里?

陈　士　杰:我想去海边,我喜欢海。

刘　　芳:你可以去海南或者青岛,这两个地方的海都很漂亮。

陈　士　杰:谢谢你的建议,你更喜欢山还是海?

刘　　芳:我也喜欢海。

陈　士　杰:那我们可以一起去。

刘　　芳:那太好了。

语法知识 Grammar

1. 选择疑问句:还是

用法:用两个或两个以上选项进行提问。

句型:A+还是+B。

例句:我们是打车去还是坐公交车去?

你是吃米饭还是吃面?

2. 连词:或者

用法:用来连接词与词表达并列关系。

句型:A+或者+B。

例句:给我打电话或者发电子邮件都可以。

上午或者晚上,我都有时间。

六 课后练习 Exercises

1. 写一写 (Writing)

根据拼音写汉字。
Write down the corresponding characters according to pinyin.

夫_____(fù)　　_____念(huái)　　_____弟(xiōng)

2. 连一连 (Matching)

把右列的汉字与左列的汉字相连组词。
Match characters in the right column with one in the left column to form a phrase.

母　　　　　　傅
师　　　　　　亲
兄　　　　　　定
规　　　　　　重
尊　　　　　　弟

3. 填一填 (Blank-filling)

用适当的汉字填空。
Fill the following blanks with proper characters.

(1) _____是爸爸的弟弟。
(2) 他教的内容很细致,是一个好_____。
(3) 只有尊重自己的人,才能_____别人。
(4) 你去学校是坐公交车_____坐校车?

4. 默一默 (Writing from memory)

根据课文内容填空。
Fill in the blanks according to the text.

乐殊_____,礼别尊卑。上和_____,夫唱妇随。
外受傅训,入奉_____。诸姑伯叔,犹子比儿。
_____兄弟,同气连枝。交友投分,切磨_____。

5. 说一说(Talking)

根据所给场景，编写对话并练习。
Based on the given situations, make dialogues and practice.
你喜欢参加朋友聚会吗？
提示：还是；或者

....
....
....

礼　乐

　　礼乐是中国文化的代名词，中国传统文化的表现形式可以用礼乐来概(gài)括。广义的"礼"是中国文化的统称，包括了哲(zhé)学(xué)、政治、社会、教育等所有的文化内容。狭(xiá)义的"礼"指社会秩(zhì)序(xù)，"乐"则是指舞蹈和音乐，礼乐则是指传统的教化手段，用来维护社会的稳定秩序。

　　Rites and music are synonymous with Chinese culture, and the expressions of traditional Chinese culture can be included by rites and music. "Rites", in the broad sense, is a generic term for Chinese culture, which includes all cultural contents, such as philosophy, politics, society and education, etc. "Rites", in the narrow sense, refers to the social order. "Music" refers to dance and music. Rites and music together refer to the traditional means of indoctrination, which are used to maintain a stable social order.

第十课　仁慈隐恻

Lesson Ten　Mercy and Sympathy

1. 描红并注音(Trace strokes and add pinyin)

( )
仁

( )
义

( )
性

( )
心

( )
好

( )
自

2. 话题导入(Topic introduction)

你有对一件事物非常沉迷的时候吗？谈谈你的经历和感受。

Have you ever been very addicted to something? Tell us about your experience and feelings.

Rén cí yǐn cè① zào cì② fú③ lí
仁 慈 隐 恻 ， 造 次 弗 离 。

Jié yì lián tuì diān pèi fěi④ kuī
节 义 廉 退 ， 颠 沛 匪 亏 。

Xìng jìng qíng yì xīn dòng shén pí
性 静 情 逸 ， 心 动 神 疲 。

Shǒu zhēn zhì mǎn zhú wù yì yí
守 真 志 满 ， 逐 物 意 移 。

Jiān chí yǎ cāo⑤ hǎo jué⑥ zì mí⑦
坚 持 雅 操 ， 好 爵 自 縻 。

1. 注释(Notes)

①隐恻：恻隐，见到别人遭遇不幸，心中感到难过(feel grieved when seeing others suffering from unfortunate things)。

②造次：仓促、匆忙(hurried, hasty)。

③弗：不要(do not, will not)。

④匪：不可以(cannot, should not)。

⑤操：操守,德行(virtue)。

⑥爵：酒杯(goblet)，此处引申为"职位(position)、运气(luck)"。

⑦縻：本意为绳子(rope)，此处用作动词，意为"捆绑"(tie up)。

2. 原文大意(Paraphrase)

我们在仓促危急时也不能抛离仁义、慈爱和恻隐之心。

气节、正义、廉洁、谦让的美德，在最穷困潦倒时也不可亏缺。

品性沉静淡泊，情绪就会安逸自在；内心浮躁好动，精神就会疲惫困倦。

保持自己天生的善性，愿望就可以得到满足；追求物欲享受，善性就会转移改变。

坚定地保持高雅情操，好的职位自然就会属于你。

三 汉字学习 Chinese character

拼音	yì
词性	名词(n.)
释义	公正合理的道理(righteousness)
搭配	含义(meaning)
例句	这个词有四种含义。 The word has four meanings.

退

拼音	tuì
词性	动词(v.)
释义	向后走(walk backward)
搭配	退步(regress)；退休(retire)
例句	最近我的英文在急剧退步。 My English has been dramatically regressing recently.

性

拼音	xìng
词性	名词(n.)
释义	人的品格(personality)；特质(nature)
搭配	个性(characteristic)
例句	每个人都有自己的个性特点。 Everyone has his own characteristics.

神

拼音	shén

词性	名词(n.);形容词(adj.)
释义	状态(spirit);意识(consciousness)
搭配	精神(spirit);留神(watch out for)
例句	要想成功,必须有拼搏的精神。 If you want to succeed, you must have the spirit of struggle.

志

拼音	zhì
词性	名词(n.)
释义	人的目标和意向(goal and will)
搭配	杂志(magazine);志愿者(volunteer)
例句	这些志愿者都是最可爱、最美丽的人! These volunteers are the most lovely and beautiful people!

守

拼音	shǒu
词性	动词(v.)
释义	保护(protect)
搭配	遵守(follow, abide by)
例句	我们应该遵守学校的规定。 We should abide by the rules of the school.

逐

拼音	zhú
词性	动词(v.)
释义	追赶(run after)
搭配	逐渐,逐步(gradually);驱逐(deport)

例句	设定闹钟有助于逐步养成守时的习惯。 Setting an alarm clock helps to gradually develop the habit of punctuality.

移

拼音	yí
词性	动词(v.)
释义	使物体改变位置(move something elsewhere)
搭配	移动(move);移民(immigrate, immigrant)
例句	中国移民的数量有上升的趋势。 The number of Chinese immigrants is on the rise.

坚

拼音	jiān
词性	形容词(adj.)
释义	硬(hard);不容易坏的(firm)
搭配	坚强(strong);坚持(insist)
例句	这个孩子的意志变得更加坚强了。 The child's will became even stronger.

操

拼音	cāo
词性	动词(v.)
释义	掌握(control);训练(drill)
搭配	操场(playground);操心(worry about)
例句	操场就在教室的窗外。 The sports ground is right outside the classroom window.

四 日常对话 Dialogue

（一）怎么去学校（How to get to school）

刘芳：你每天怎么去学校？
　　　Liú Fāng Nǐ měi tiān zěn me qù xué xiào

李华：我骑车上学，你呢？
　　　Lǐ Huá Wǒ qí chē shàng xué nǐ ne

刘芳：我走路上学。
　　　Liú Fāng Wǒ zǒu lù shàng xué

李华：走这么远你一定很累吧。
　　　Lǐ Huá Zǒu zhè me yuǎn nǐ yí dìng hěn lèi ba

刘芳：还好。我喜欢走路，常走路精神好。
　　　Liú Fāng Hái hǎo Wǒ xǐ huan zǒu lù cháng zǒu lù jīng shen hǎo

李华：说得对，我明天也走路去学校。
　　　Lǐ huá Shuō de duì wǒ míng tiān yě zǒu lù qù xué xiào

（二）课后运动（After-class activities）

李华：刘芳，待会儿和我一起跑步吗？
　　　Lǐ Huá Liú Fāng dāi huìr hé wǒ yì qǐ pǎo bù ma

刘芳：对不起，我要去跳健身操。
　　　Liú Fāng Duì bu qǐ wǒ yào qù tiào jiàn shēn cāo

李华：健身操？怪不得你看起来这么有精神。
　　　Lǐ Huá Jiàn shēn cāo guài bu de nǐ kàn qǐ lái zhè me yǒu jīng shen

刘芳：是啊，我每周都坚持跳呢。
　　　Liú Fāng Shì a wǒ měi zhōu dōu jiān chí tiào ne

李华：有空我也在家试试。
　　　Lǐ Huá Yǒu kòng wǒ yě zài jiā shì shi

刘芳：好啊，等你学会了我们一起跳。
　　　Liú Fāng Hǎo a děng nǐ xué huì le wǒ men yì qǐ tiào

五 语法知识 Grammar

1. 疑问句：怎么

用法：提出问题、询问情况。

句型：主语＋怎么＋动词＋（语气词）？

例句：这个题目怎么做？

　　　你每天怎么上学？

2. 连动句

用法:连动句是用连动短语充当谓语的句子,或者是由连动短语直接构成的句子。

句型:主语＋动词1＋动词2。

例句:张丽丽去图书馆看书。

　　　李华走路上学。

 课后练习 Exercises

1. 写一写(Writing)

根据拼音写汉字。

Write down the corresponding characters according to pinyin.

　　chí　　　　　　wù　　　　　　mǎn
坚＿＿＿　　　＿＿＿品　　　＿＿＿足

2. 连一连(Matching)

把右列的汉字与左列的汉字相连组词。

Match characters in the right column with one in the left column to form a phrase.

满　　　　　　　　　　持
安　　　　　　　　　　足
坚　　　　　　　　　　品
文　　　　　　　　　　物
物　　　　　　　　　　情
心　　　　　　　　　　静

3. 填一填(Blank-filling)

用所给的词语填空。

Fill the following blanks with given characters.

　　　　　　　　物品　　满意　　冷静　　坚持

（1）无论遇到什么波折,我们都要(　　　)下去。

（2）如果我很(　　　),你会得到奖品。

（3）面对强大的敌人,我们要沉着(　　　)。

（4）柴米油盐是我们生活中的日常(　　　)。

千字文

4. 默一默(Writing from memory)

根据课文内容填空。
Fill in the blanks according to the text.

性静情_____,心动神疲。

守真志_____,逐物意移。

5. 说一说(Talking)

根据所给场景,编写对话并练习。
Based on the given situations, make dialogues and practice.

你爬过山吗？说一说你的经历。

....
....

七 延伸学习 Extended reading

诸葛亮的《诫子书》

诸葛亮(181—234),三国时期(220—280)的战略家,在家教方面很有造诣。《诫子书》便是他为了帮助子女成长而创作的文章。文章中写道：一个人首先要让内心安静下来,神志清醒,然后陶冶自己的性情,不受外物的干扰,不满足于微小的成绩,坚持自己伟大的志向,做一个不断进步的人,最终成就大事。

Zhuge Liang(181-234), strategist in the Three Kingdoms period(220-280), was very accomplished at home tutoring. *The Book of Commandments* is an article he wrote to help his children grow up. In this article, he said that, first of all, a person should calm down and be in his/her right senses; then, cultivate his/her own temperament, be undisturbed by external things, not satisfied with trivial achievements, stick to his/her great ambition, make progress continuously, and finally accomplish his/her mission.

第十一课　都邑华夏

Lesson Eleven　　Magnificent Ancient Capitals

1. 描红并注音(Trace strokes and add pinyin)

（　）
东

（　）
西

（　）
宫

（　）
飞

（　）
舍

（　）
画

2. 话题导入(Topic introduction)

你在哪个中国城市旅游过？谈谈你的经历。
Which Chinese city have you visited? Talk about your experience.

Dū	yì①	huá	xià	dōng	xī	èr	jīng
都	邑	华	夏 ，	东	西	二	京 。
Bèi	máng②	miàn	luò	fú	wèi	jù	jīng
背	邙	面	洛 ，	浮	渭	据	泾 。
Gōng	diàn	pán	yù	lóu	guàn	fēi	jīng
宫	殿	盘	郁 ，	楼	观	飞	惊 。
Tú③	xiě	qín	shòu	huà	cǎi	xiān	líng
图	写	禽	兽 ，	画	彩	仙	灵 。
Bǐng④	shè⑤	páng	qǐ⑥	jiǎ	zhàng	duì	yíng
丙	舍	傍	启 ，	甲	帐	对	楹 。

1. 注释(Notes)

①邑：城市(city)。

②邙：山名，北邙山，在河南省(a mountain in Henan Province)。

③图：绘画(painting)。

④丙：天干中的第三个(the third in the Ten Heavenly Stems)。

⑤舍：房屋(house, room)。

⑥启：打开(open)。

2. 原文大意(Paraphrase)

古代的都城华美壮观,有东京洛阳和西京长安。

东京洛阳背靠北邙山,南临洛水;西京长安左跨渭河,右依泾水。

宫殿盘旋曲折,重重叠叠;楼阁高耸如飞,触目惊心。

宫殿上绘着各种飞禽走兽,描画出五彩的天仙神灵。

正殿两边的配殿从侧面开启,豪华的帐幕对着高高的楹柱。

| 华 | 丿 | 亻 | 化 | 化 | 华 | 华 |

拼音	huá
词性	形容词(adj.)
释义	美丽而有光彩的(illustrious)
搭配	豪华(luxury)
例句	我们应该反对在衣着装饰上奢侈豪华、铺张浪费。 We should oppose extravagance and waste in clothing and decoration.

据

拼音	jù
词性	动词(v.)
释义	倚靠着(lean against)
搭配	根据(according to, based on)
例句	根据长期的观察，他得出了这个结论。 Based on long-term observation, he came to this conclusion.

盘

拼音	pán
词性	动词(v.)
释义	环绕(wind)
搭配	盘旋(hover)
例句	雄鹰盘旋在天空中。 The eagle hovered high in the sky.

惊

拼音	jīng
词性	动词(v.)
释义	出人意料(surprise)
搭配	吃惊(shock, surprise)

例句	这个消息公布的时候，大家都非常吃惊。 When the news was announced, everyone was very surprised.

彩

拼音	cǎi
词性	名词(n.)
释义	多种颜色(rich and bright colors)
搭配	精彩(wonderful)
例句	周末我去看了一场精彩的足球赛。 I went to watch a wonderful football match at the weekend.

舍

拼音	shè
词性	名词(n.)
释义	房屋(house, room)
搭配	宿舍(dormitory)
例句	我喜欢在宿舍看电视。 I like watching TV in the dormitory.

启

拼音	qǐ
词性	动词(v.)
释义	打开(open)
搭配	启发(inspire)
例句	这个节目给了我们很大的启发。 This program has greatly inspired us.

甲

拼音	jiǎ

词性	形容词(adj.)
释义	第一的(first)
搭配	甲等(first class);指甲(fingernail)
例句	桂林山水甲天下。 Guilin scenery is the finest under heaven.

(一) 她下周就回来了(She's coming back next week)

张丽丽：李华，今天怎么没有看见王老师？
(Zhāng Lì li: Lǐ Huá, Jīn tiān zěn me méi yǒu kàn jiàn Wáng lǎo shī)

李华：王老师生病了。
(Lǐ Huá: Wáng lǎo shī shēng bìng le)

张丽丽：那王老师今天就不能给我们上课了？
(Zhāng Lì li: Nà Wáng lǎo shī jīn tiān jiù bù néng gěi wǒ men shàng kè le)

李华：是的，今天周老师会给我们上课。
(Lǐ Huá: Shì de, jīn tiān Zhōu lǎo shī huì gěi wǒ men shàng kè)

张丽丽：那王老师什么时候回来？
(Zhāng Lì li: Nà Wáng lǎo shī shén me shí hou huí lai)

李华：她下周就回来了！
(Lǐ Huá: Tā xià zhōu jiù huí lai le)

(二) 我没有哥哥高(I'm not so tall as my elder brother)

张丽丽：李华，他的书包和你的书包一样。
(Zhāng Lì li: Lǐ Huá, tā de shū bāo hé nǐ de shū bāo yí yàng)

李华：是的，他是我的哥哥。
(Lǐ Huá: Shì de, tā shì wǒ de gē ge)

张丽丽：你和你的哥哥已经一样高了。
(Zhāng Lì li: Nǐ hé nǐ de gē ge yǐ jīng yí yàng gāo le)

李华：没有，我还没有哥哥高，我比他矮一点儿。
(Lǐ Huá: Méi yǒu, wǒ hái méi yǒu gē ge gāo, wǒ bǐ tā ǎi yì diǎnr)

张丽丽：你哥哥的成绩和你一样好吧？
(Zhāng Lì li: Nǐ gē ge de chéng jì hé nǐ yí yàng hǎo ba)

李华：我哥哥更优秀。
(Lǐ Huá: Wǒ gē ge gèng yōu xiù)

千字文

五 语法知识 Grammar

1. 时间副词：就

用法：表示事情在短期内即将发生。

例句：我一会儿就去扫地。

妈妈下班后就会来接我放学。

2. 比较句：

用法：A和B一样/不一样＋形容词，表示A和B两者相比较，结果相同或不相同，后面也可以加上形容词表示比较的某一方面。表示否定时还可用"没有＋A＋形容词"。

例句：这棵树和那棵树一样高。

你的裙子和丽丽的一样漂亮。

我的书包和哥哥的不一样。

我的汉字写得没有姐姐的好。

六 课后练习 Exercises

1. 写一写(Writing)

根据拼音写汉字。

Write down the corresponding characters according to pinyin.

  jù   cǎi   huá   pán

根____ 精____ 豪____ ____旋

2. 连一连(Matching)

把右列的汉字与左列的汉字相连组词。

Match characters in the right column with one in the left column to form a phrase.

甲   舍

宿   等

启   惊

吃   发

3. 填一填(Blank-filling)

用所给的词语填空。

Fill the following blanks with given characters.

吃惊　　盘旋　　精彩　　根据

(1) (　　)这些证据,可以确定就是他做的这件事。

(2) 这个消息对我们每个人来说都非常(　　)。

(3) 周末,我们去剧院看了一场(　　)的表演。

(4) 车队沿山路(　　)而上。

4. 默一默(Writing from memory)

根据课文内容填空。

Fill in the blanks according to the text.

都邑_____夏,东西二京。

宫殿盘郁,楼观飞_____。

图写禽兽,画_____仙灵。

5. 说一说(Talking)

根据提示,编写对话并练习。

Based on the given tips, make dialogues and practice.

比较一下你和你的兄弟姐妹(如长相、爱好、性格等)。

七 延伸学习 Extended reading

故　宫

故宫位于北京市中心,也称"紫(zǐ)禁(jìn)城",位于北京中轴(zhóu)线的中心。这里曾居住过24个皇帝,是明清两代的皇宫,现为"故宫博(bó)物院"。故宫于明成祖永乐四年(1406年)开始建设,到永乐十八年(1420年)建成。

故宫的整个建筑金碧(bì)辉(huī)煌(huáng),庄严绚(xuàn)丽(yù),被誉为世界五大宫之一。故宫的宫殿建筑是中国现存最大、最完整的古建筑群,气魄宏伟,极为壮观。故宫博物院收藏有大量古代艺术珍品,是中国收藏文物最丰富的博物馆,也是世界著名的古代文化艺术博物馆。

故宫是国家5A级旅游景区,1961年被列为第一批全国重点文物保护单位,1987年被列为世界文化遗产。

The Palace Museum, situated in the heart of Beijing, also known as the "Forbidden City", is in the center of Beijing's central axis. Twenty-four emperors once lived here and it was the palace of the Ming and Qing Dynasties. Now it is the "Palace Museum". The building of the Palace Museum began in 1406 and was completed in 1420.

The whole building of the Forbidden City is resplendent, solemn and gorgeous, known as one of the five great palaces in the world. The palace buildings in the Forbidden City are the largest and most complete ancient buildings in China. They are magnificent and spectacular. The Palace Museum houses a large collection of ancient art treasures. It is the most abundant museum in China and the world-famous museum of ancient culture and art.

The Palace Museum is a national 5A scenic area. It was listed as the first batch of national key cultural relics protection units in 1961 and world cultural heritage in 1987.

第十二课　肆筵设席

Lesson Twelve　Banquet and Music

1. 描红并注音(Trace strokes and add pinyin)

( )
吹

( )
星

( )
右

( )
左

( )
明

( )
典

2. 话题导入（Topic introduction）

你知道中国的"新四大发明"是什么吗？

Do you know what is China's "New Four Inventions"?

肆筵设席，鼓瑟吹笙①。
Sì yán shè xí, gǔ sè chuī shēng②。

升阶纳陛，弁转疑星。
Shēng jiē nà bì③, biàn④ zhuǎn yí xīng。

右通广内，左达承明。
Yòu tōng guǎng nèi⑤, zuǒ dá chéng míng。

既集《坟》《典》，亦聚群英。
Jì jí fén diǎn⑥, yì jù qún yīng。

杜稿钟隶，漆书壁经。
Dù gǎo Zhōng lì, qī shū bì jīng。

1. 注释（Notes）

①筵：酒席（feast）。

②笙：一种竹管乐器（a musical instrument made of bamboo pipes）。

③陛：帝王宫殿的台阶（steps of an imperial palace）。

④弁：古代男子戴的一种帽子（a kind of hat worn by men in ancient times）。

⑤广内：帝王书库（the imperial family's private library）。

⑥《坟》《典》：《三坟》与《五典》（two books recording the deeds of Chinese emperors）。

2. 原文大意（Paraphrase）

宫殿中大摆宴席，乐人吹笙鼓瑟，一片歌舞升平的景象。

登上台阶进入殿堂的文武百官，珠帽转动，像满天的星斗。

右面通向藏有书籍的广内殿，左面到达朝臣休息的承明殿。

这里收藏了很多的典籍名著，也聚集着成群的文武英才。

书殿中有杜度的草书、钟繇的隶书，还有漆写的古籍和孔子故宅墙壁内的经典。

设　丶　讠　计　讠　识　设　设

拼音	shè
词性	动词(v.)
释义	安排(arrange)
搭配	设计(design)
例句	迈克负责整个工程的设计工作。 Mike is responsible for designing the entire project.

席

拼音	xí
词性	名词(n.)
释义	座位(seat)
搭配	主席(chairperson)
例句	他是一个大型国际组织的主席。 He's the chairman of a large international organization.

鼓

拼音	gǔ
词性	动词(v.)
释义	弹奏(play)
搭配	鼓励(encourage)
例句	她的父母鼓励她好好学习。 Her parents encouraged her in her studies.

升

拼音	shēng
词性	动词(v.)

释义	登,上(ascend)
搭配	晋升(promotion)
例句	如果有合适的技能,就有很好的晋升机会。There are good opportunities for promotion if you have the right skills.

阶 了 阝 阝' 阶 阶 阶

拼音	jiē
词性	名词(n.)
释义	梯子(staircase)
搭配	台阶(stair, step)
例句	他慢慢爬上台阶。He climbed up the stairs slowly.

转 一 t 车 车 车 轩 转 转

拼音	zhuǎn
词性	动词(v.)
释义	改换方向(change directions)
搭配	转变(turn, change)
例句	通过努力,我成功转变了大家对我的看法。I managed to change people's perception of me through hard work.

疑 ⺁ ⺊ ヒ ヒ ヒ 矣 矣 矣 疑 疑 疑 疑 疑

拼音	yí
词性	动词(v.)
释义	迷惑(puzzle)

搭配	疑问(question)
例句	如果有疑问,请及时和我们联系。 Please duly contact us should you have any questions.

拼音	nèi
词性	名词(n.)
释义	里面(inside)
搭配	内容(content)
例句	章节标题有助于学生了解书的内容。 The chapter headings are useful for students to understand the content of the book.

拼音	dá
词性	动词(v.)
释义	到(reach)
搭配	到达(reach)
例句	我们将在两点钟到达北京。 We will reach Beijing at 2 o'clock.

拼音	chéng
词性	动词(v.)
释义	捧着(support with palms, bear)
搭配	承担(undertake)
例句	我们要勇于承担责任。 We should have the courage to undertake the responsibility.

既 ㄱ ㄱ ㅋ 目 目 臣 旣 旣 既

拼音	jì
词性	连词（conj.）
释义	已经（already）；与"又"连用（both…and）
搭配	既成事实（fait accompli）；既快又好（fast and well）
例句	他生病是既成事实。His illness is a fait accompli. 她做事真是既快又好。She works really fast and well.

集 ノ イ イ 亻 仁 伫 佯 佯 隹 隼 集

拼音	jí
词性	动词（v.）
释义	收藏（collect）
搭配	集合（gather, assemble）
例句	全体学生明天在教室集合。 All the students will assemble in the classroom tomorrow.

聚 一 丆 ㄇ 月 耳 取 取 取 取 聚

聚 聚 聚

拼音	jù
词性	动词（v.）
释义	会合（gather）
搭配	聚会（get together; party）
例句	我们正在举办她的生日聚会。 We are throwing a party for her birthday.

群

拼音	qún
词性	名词(n.)
释义	集体(crowd, group)
搭配	群众(the masses)
例句	从群众中来,到群众中去。From the masses, to the masses.

壁

拼音	bì
词性	名词(n.)
释义	墙(wall)
搭配	隔壁(next door)
例句	隔壁的音乐声打扰了她的思绪。 Music from the next door obtruded upon her thoughts.

四 日常对话 Dialogue

(一) 拜访朋友 (Visiting friends)

李 华：丽丽,我已经到楼下了,你家在几楼呀?
Lǐ Huá: Lì li, wǒ yǐ jīng dào lóu xià le, nǐ jiā zài jǐ lóu ya

张丽丽：我家在十楼。
Zhāng Lì li: Wǒ jiā zài shí lóu

李 华：这么高呀,我乘电梯上来吧。
Lǐ Huá: Zhè me gāo ya, wǒ chéng diàn tī shàng lai ba

张丽丽：今天电梯好像坏了。
Zhāng Lì li: Jīn tiān diàn tī hǎo xiàng huài le

李　　华：真的吗？我看一下。好像真的坏了，那我只能走上来了。

张丽丽：真是辛苦你了。

李　　华：没关系，我正好锻炼一下。

（二）爬山（Climbing mountains）

刘　　芳：今天天气真好呀，非常适合爬山！

陈士杰：是啊，我们一起爬上去吧。

刘　　芳：好呀，我正担心我一个人爬不上去呢。

陈士杰：不用害怕，感觉累了我们可以休息一会儿。

刘　　芳：好的，山上的风景一定很不错。

陈士杰：是的，所以我们一定要努力爬到山顶，加油。

刘　　芳：加油！

五、语法知识 Grammar

1. 趋向补语：上来

用法：表示由低到高，动作方向朝着说话人所在地的方向。

句型：主语＋动词＋上来。

例句：他走上来。

　　　她朝着山顶爬上来。

2. 趋向补语：上去

用法：表示由低到高，动作方向朝着说话人以外的方向。

句型：主语＋动词＋上去。

例句：你走上去吧。

　　　她跳了上去。

1. 写一写(Writing)

根据拼音写汉字。

Write down the corresponding characters according to pinyin.

Zhuǎn	jí	chéng	dá
＿＿变	＿＿合	＿＿担	到＿＿

2. 连一连(Matching)

把右列的汉字与左列的汉字相连组词。

Match characters in the right column with one in the left column to form a phrase.

既　　　　　　　　　会
聚　　　　　　　　　计
承　　　　　　　　　问
鼓　　　　　　　　　然
疑　　　　　　　　　励
设　　　　　　　　　受

3. 填一填(Blank-filling)

用适当的汉字填空。

Fill the following blanks with proper characters.

（1）失败是通往成功道路上必经的＿＿＿＿段。
（2）写作是表＿＿＿＿情感的一种好方法。
（3）我还不太理解这堂课上老师所讲的＿＿＿＿容，可以向您请教吗？
（4）地球围绕着太阳旋＿＿＿＿。
（5）老师在操场上呼唤同学们＿＿＿＿合。
（6）他大胆地向老师提出了自己的＿＿＿＿问。

4. 默一默(Writing from memory)

根据课文内容填空。

Fill in the blanks according to the text.

肆筵＿＿　＿＿，＿＿瑟吹笙。
＿＿＿＿　纳陛，弁＿＿＿＿星。
右通广＿＿，左＿＿＿＿明。

_____ _____《坟》《典》,亦_____ _____英。

杜稿钟隶,漆书_____经。

5. 说一说(Talking)

根据所给场景,编写对话并练习。

Based on the given situations, make dialogues and practice.

你的班级周末组织爬山活动,试试编写一组在爬山时候的对话。

提示:趋向补语的用法(动词+上来;动词+上去)

七 延伸学习 Extended reading

鸿 门 宴 (hóng mén yàn)

公元前206年,刘邦(bāng)先入关灭秦(miè qín),进驻咸阳(zhù xián),并派兵把守(pài shǒu)函谷(hán gǔ)关,以对抗(kàng)项羽(xiàng yǔ)的西进。项羽率领(shuài lǐng)40万大军到达(dá)后,攻破(gōng pò)函谷关,进驻鸿(hóng)门,准备袭击(xí jī)刘邦。

刘邦知道实力悬殊(xuán shū),采纳(cǎi nà)张良的建议(jiàn yì),结交(jiāo)了项羽的叔父项伯,希望从中给予调解(yǔ tiáo jiě),以作缓(huǎn)兵之计(jì),并且亲自到鸿门和项羽见面。

宴(yàn)会上,项羽的谋(móu)士范增让项庄舞剑(jiàn),意图刺杀(cì shā)刘邦。项伯已被收(shōu)买,于是也连忙拔(lián máng bá)剑起舞,用自己掩护(yǎn hù)住刘邦。而刘邦的部将樊哙(bù jiàng fán kuài)(大将军)带剑执盾(zhí dùn)闯入来保护刘邦。后来,刘邦找借口匆忙离去。

In 206 B.C., Liu Bang first crossed the pass to overthrow the Qin Dynasty and stationed in Xianyang. He also sent troops to guard Hangu pass to resist Xiang Yu's westward advance. Xiang Yu led a troop of 400,000 soldiers and broke through Hangu pass and stationed himself in Hongmen, preparing to attack Liu Bang.

Liu Bang, aware of the great disparity in military strength, took Zhang Liang's advice and befriended Xiang Bo, Xiang Yu's uncle, expecting Xiang Bo to mediate between him and Xiang Yu so as to slow down the war. He also went to Hongmen himself to meet Xiang Yu.

At the banquet, Fan Zeng, Xiang Yu's counselor, asked Xiang Zhuang to dance with a sword, intending to assassinate Liu Bang. Xiang Bo, who had been bribed, quickly drew out his sword and joined the dance to cover Liu Bang. Fan Kuai, one of Liu Bang's generals, broke into the banquet with his sword and shield to protect Liu Bang. Later, Liu Bang made an excuse and left hurriedly.

第十三课　府罗将相

Lesson Thirteen　Generals and Ministers

1. 描红并注音(Trace strokes and add pinyin)

2. 话题导入(Topic introduction)

谈谈你的国家有哪些主要出行方式？

What are the main modes of traveling in your country?

学习原文 Text

Fǔ luó jiàng xiàng, lù jiā① huái② qīng③。
府　罗　将　相　，路　侠　槐　卿　。

Hù fēng④ bā xiàn, jiā jǐ qiān bīng。
户　封　八　县　，家　给　千　兵　。

Gāo guān⑤ péi niǎn⑥, qū gǔ⑦ zhèn yīng⑧。
高　冠　陪　辇　，驱　毂　振　缨　。

Shì lù⑨ chǐ fù, chē jià féi qīng。
世　禄　侈　富　，车　驾　肥　轻　。

Cè gōng mào shí, lè bēi⑩ kè míng⑪。
策　功　茂　实　，勒　碑　刻　铭　。

1. 注释(Notes)

①侠：同"夹"(place in between)。

②槐：槐树(Chinese scholar tree)。

③卿：高级官员(senior official)。

④封：帝王把爵位(有时连土地)或称号赐给臣子(Emperors granted titles and/or land to their ministers)。

⑤冠：帽子(hat)。

⑥辇：用人拉或推的车(a cart pulled or pushed by people)。

⑦毂：车轮的中心部分，这里指车(the hub of a wheel; here referring to a carriage)。

⑧缨：绳子(rope)。

⑨禄：官员的工资(salary)。

⑩碑：刻着图文、用于纪念或标记的、竖立的石头(stele, a stone tablet)。

⑪铭：器物、碑等上面记录事实、功德等的文字(the writing on utensils, steles, etc. to record facts, merits, etc.)。

2. 原文大意(Paraphrase)

宫廷内将相依次排成两列，宫廷外大夫公卿夹道站立。

他们每家都有八县之广的封地，还有上千名的侍卫。

戴着高大帽子的官员们陪着皇帝出游，驾着车马，帽带飘舞着，非常威风。

他们的子孙世代领受俸禄,奢侈富有,出门时驾着轻车肥马。朝廷详尽地记载他们的功德,刻在碑石上以便流传后世。

三 汉字学习 Chinese character

千字文

府

拼音	fǔ
词性	名词(n.)
释义	指某些国家元首办公或居住的地方(the place where heads of states work or live)
搭配	王府(palace);政府(government)
例句	他是一名政府官员。 He is a government official.

将

拼音	jiāng;jiàng
词性	名词(n.)
释义	军衔名(military rank title);将领(military officer)
搭配	将军(general);即将(nearly)
例句	不想当将军的士兵不是好士兵。 A soldier who does not want to be a general is not a good soldier.

户

拼音	hù
词性	名词(n.)
释义	人家(family);门(door)
搭配	窗户(windows);门户(gateway;portal)
例句	这是一个简便易用的门户网站。 This is an easy-to-use portal website.

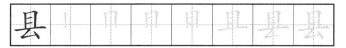

拼音	xiàn
词性	名词(n.)
释义	中国省级以下的一种行政区划(an administrative division below the provincial level in China)
搭配	县城(county town)
例句	我来自江苏省的一个小县城。 I come from a small county town in Jiangsu Province.

拼音	bīng
词性	名词(n.)
释义	战士(soldier);军队(army)
搭配	士兵(soldier);民兵(militia)
例句	孩子们正在玩当士兵的游戏。 The children were playing soldiers.

拼音	péi
词性	动词(v.)
释义	跟随在一起,伴随(accompany)
搭配	陪伴,陪同(accompany)
例句	我今天要陪妈妈去医院。 I will accompany my mother to the hospital.

拼音	zhèn
词性	动词(v.)

释义	摇动(shake);挥动(brandish)
搭配	振动(vibrate);振作(cheer up)
例句	他帮助我振作起来。 He helped me cheer up.

世 一 十 廿 世

拼音	shì
词性	名词(n.)
释义	人的一生(lifetime)
搭配	逝世(die, pass away);一生一世(one's whole life)
例句	他一生一世都爱着她。 He loved her in his whole life.

驾 ᄀ 力 加 加 驾 驾 驾

拼音	jià
词性	动词(v.)
释义	使牲口拉车(to cause animals to pull carriages)
搭配	驾驶(drive);酒驾(drunk driving)
例句	酒后千万不能驾驶汽车。 Never drive after drinking.

肥 丿 月 月 月 肥 肥 肥

拼音	féi
词性	形容词(adj.)
释义	胖的(fat)
搭配	肥胖(fat);减肥(lose weight)
例句	她不吃晚饭,因为她正在减肥。 She doesn't eat dinner because she is losing weight.

策 丿 ㄅ ㅂ 竺 竺 笁 笁 筞 第 策

策

拼音	cè
词性	动词(v.);名词(n.)
释义	谋划(scheme);计谋、办法(method)
搭配	策划(plan);对策(countermeasure)
例句	这个问题你有什么对策吗? Do you have a countermeasure to this problem?

功 一 丆 工 功 功

拼音	gōng
词性	名词(n.)
释义	成绩(achievement)
搭配	功劳(contribution);成功(success)
例句	他的成功激励了其他人。His success inspired other people.

四 日常对话 Dialogue

(一) 我以前看过这部电影 (I saw this movie before)

张丽丽:李华,今天王老师要给我们放一部电影。

李华:你知道是什么电影吗?

张丽丽:好像是《中国机长》。

李华:我看过这部电影,你看过吗?

张丽丽:我没看过。不过,据说很好看。

李华:没错,是一部非常精彩的电影!

(二)打篮球 (Play basketball)

刘　芳：丽丽,下午出来玩吗?

张丽丽：好啊,可是我正在写作业。

刘　芳：李华他们在打篮球呢,一起去看看吧!

张丽丽：好的,等我写完作业,我就过去。

刘　芳：好的,那我在篮球场等你。

张丽丽：好,一会儿见。

五 语法知识 Grammar

1. 时态助词(过)

用法:表示某个动作或变化已经成为过去。

比较:了,表示某个动作或变化已经完成。

句型:主语+动词+过+宾语。

例句:我已经学过了这篇课文。

我吃过饭了。

2. 动作状态(在……呢)

用法:正在,表示动作正在发生,某人正在做某件事情。

句型:主语+在+(名词)+动词+呢!

例句:爸爸在客厅里看电视呢!

我正在食堂吃饭呢。

六 课后练习 Exercises

1. 写一写(Writing)

根据拼音写汉字。

Write down the corresponding characters according to pinyin.

gōng　　　　　péi　　　　　fù
＿＿绩　　　　＿＿伴　　　　＿＿裕

2．连一连(Matching)

把右列的汉字与左列的汉字相连组词。

Match characters in the right column with one in the left column to form a phrase.

陪　　　　　　　　　　有
雕　　　　　　　　　　车
驾　　　　　　　　　　刻
富　　　　　　　　　　胖
肥　　　　　　　　　　同

3．填一填(Blank-filling)

用所给的词语填空。

Fill the following blanks with given characters.

　　　　　陪同　　肥胖　　功德　　雕刻　　住户

（1）这里的(　　　)都非常热情,总邀请我去他们家玩。
（2）明天我要(　　　)妈妈去医院检查身体。
（3）这个(　　　)艺术品真好看。
（4）这位慈善家的(　　　)名扬天下。
（5）我国的(　　　)病人正在逐年增加。

4．默一默(Writing from memory)

根据课文内容填空。

Fill in the blanks according to the text.

＿＿＿封＿＿＿县,家给＿＿＿＿＿。
＿＿＿冠＿＿＿华,驱毂＿＿＿缨。
＿＿＿禄侈＿＿＿,＿＿＿驾＿＿＿＿＿。
策＿＿＿茂＿＿＿,勒碑＿＿＿铭。

5．说一说(Talking)

根据所给场景,编写对话并练习。

Based on the given situations, make dialogues and practice.

你上个周末做了什么？有什么让你特别难忘的经历吗？

提示:过、了

中国的新四大发明

"高铁、扫码支付、共享单车和网购"被称作中国的新四大发明。

"高铁"在中国的发展十分迅速,极大地丰富了人们的出行方式。中国已经成为世界上高速铁路建设运营规模最大、技术最全面、管理经验最丰富的国家。

"扫码支付"是二维码在消费领域的广泛应用,极大地方便了人们的生活。

"共享单车"是一种新型共享经济。它帮助人们缩短出行时间,提高效率。

随着通信和交通的发展,因为方便快捷和省时省力,"网购"成了当下越来越多人的选择。

"CRH(China Railway Highspeed), QR code scanning payment, bike-sharing and online shopping" are together referred to as four new inventions in China.

The rapid development of CRH has greatly facilitated people's mobility in China. With regard to highspeed railway, China has the largest construction and operation scale, the most comprehensive technology and the most experienced management in the world.

"QR code scanning payment" is the extensive application of QR in the consumption field and has tremendously improved people's life.

"Bike-sharing" is a new type of sharing economy, which has helped people shorten their time spent in travelling around and improved their efficiency.

With the development of communication and transportation, because of its convenience and timeliness, "online shopping" has become the choice of more and more people.

第十四课　磻溪伊尹

Lesson Fourteen　Jiang Ziya and Yi Yin

1. 描红并注音(Trace strokes and add pinyin)

( )
时

( )
宅

( )
旦

( )
回

( )
说

( )
多

2. 话题导入(Topic introduction)

你知道伯乐的意思吗?

Do you know the meaning of "Bo Le" in Chinese?

Pán xī ① Yī Yǐn② zuǒ shí ē héng③
磻 溪 伊 尹 , 佐 时 阿 衡 。

Yǎn zhái④ Qū fù wēi Dàn⑤ shú yíng
奄 宅 曲 阜 , 微 旦 孰 营 。

Huán gōng kuāng⑥ hé jì ruò fú qīng
桓 公 匡 合 , 济 弱 扶 倾 。

Qǐ⑦ huí hàn Huì Yuè⑧ gǎn Wǔ Dīng⑨
绮 回 汉 惠 , 说 感 武 丁 。

Jùn yì⑩ mì wù⑪ duō shì shí⑫ níng
俊 乂 密 勿 , 多 士 寔 宁 。

1. 注释(Notes)

①磻溪:渭水河畔的一个溪潭(a brook by the Weishui River)。

②伊尹:辅佐商汤王的大臣(a minister of the Shang Dynasty)。

③阿衡:商朝官名,宰相(the title of an official in the Shang Dynasty, prime minister)。

④奄:商朝诸侯国之一。宅:指都城(one of the vassal states of the Shang Dynasty; refer to the capital here)。

⑤微:要不是(if not)。旦:指周公,西周政治家(a statesman of the Western Zhou Dynasty)。

⑥匡:端正,纠正(correct)。

⑦绮:绮里季,"商山四皓"之一(Qiliji, a scholar at the end of the Qin Dynasty)。

⑧说:指傅说,商朝贤臣(Fu Yue, a statesman of the Shang Dynasty)。

⑨武丁:商朝君主(Wuding, king of the Shang Dynasty)。

⑩俊乂:指人才(talents)。

⑪密勿:勤勉努力(diligently)。

⑫寔:通假字,通"是",有"此"的意思(this)。

2. 原文大意(Paraphrase)

周文王磻溪遇到了姜子牙,商汤王封辅佐他的伊尹为宰相。

曲阜是古奄国的都城,只有周公旦才配治理。

齐桓公匡正天下,帮助弱小的国家,扶植将要倾覆的周王室。

绮里季等"商山四皓"帮扶了汉惠帝,商君武丁因梦得到了贤相傅说。

贤俊英才勤勉努力,济济人才使得天下太平安定。

汉字学习 Chinese character

阿

拼音	ā;ē
词性	词的前缀(prefix)
释义	加在称呼上的词头(a prefix added to a title)
搭配	阿姨(aunt);东阿(Dong'e, place name)
例句	他的阿姨长得非常漂亮。 His aunt is very beautiful.

曲

拼音	qū
词性	名词(n.)
释义	曲阜,山东西南部的城市(Qufu, a city in the southwest of Shandong Province)
搭配	弯曲(winding)
例句	这是一条十分弯曲的路。 This is a winding road.

微

拼音	wēi
词性	形容词(adj.);副词(adv.)

释义	少(tiny)；无,没有(without)
搭配	细微(subtle)；微笑(smile)
例句	他什么也没说,只是微笑地看着我。 He said nothing, but smiled at me.

旦 丨 日 日 旦

拼音	dàn
词性	名词(n.)
释义	古代人名(A person's name in ancient China)；早晨(morning)；一天(day)
搭配	旦暮(morning and evening, a short time)；元旦(New Year's Day))
例句	一月一日是元旦。 January 1st is the New Year's Day.

营 一 十 艹 艹 艹 带 带 带 营 营

拼音	yíng
词性	动词(v.)
释义	建设(construction)
搭配	营业(open；business)
例句	这家超市二十四小时营业。 This supermarket is open 24 hours.

济 丶 冫 氵 汀 汸 济 济 济

拼音	jì
词性	动词(v.)
释义	帮助(help)
搭配	经济(economy)
例句	经济发展对一个国家来说非常重要。 Economic development is very important for a country.

弱

拼音	ruò
词性	形容词(adj.)
释义	力气小(weak)
搭配	弱点(weakness)
例句	脾气差是他最大的弱点。 Bad temper is his greatest weakness.

扶

拼音	fú
词性	动词(v.)
释义	搀,用手支持人或物(to support a person or thing with your hands)
搭配	搀扶(support sb. with one's hands);扶持(support)
例句	小明搀扶着爷爷过马路。 Xiaoming helped his grandfather to cross the road.

惠

拼音	huì
词性	形容词(adj.)
释义	恩典(grace);好处(benefit)
搭配	优惠(discount)
例句	这家餐厅给新顾客减价优惠。 The restaurant is offering discounts to new customers.

武

拼音	wǔ

词性	名词(n.);形容词(adj.)
释义	古帝王名(name of an emperor in ancient China);军事的(military);武术的(martial)
搭配	武器(weapon);武术(martial arts)
例句	他是一个武术教练。He is a coach of martial arts.

密

拼音	mì
词性	形容词(adj.)
释义	空隙小(thick)
搭配	亲密(intimate);密切(close)
例句	我们通过密切联系加深了了解。 We got to know each other better through close contact.

士

拼音	shì
词性	名词(n.)
释义	古代的官职名称(an official title in ancient China)
搭配	女士(lady);男士(gentleman)
例句	那位女士穿着十分优雅。The lady was very elegantly dressed.

宁

拼音	níng
词性	形容词(adj.)
释义	安定(stable)
搭配	宁可(rather)
例句	我宁可饿着肚子,也不愿意吃油炸食品。 I'd rather go hungry than eat fried food.

（一）天气（Weather）

刘　芳：最近天气越来越冷了！

陈士杰：是的，因为冬天快到了！

刘　芳：那我们要多穿些衣服。

陈士杰：是的，这样我们就不会生病。

刘　芳：那冬天有什么有意思的活动吗？

陈士杰：我们可以堆雪人、打雪仗、滑冰啊。

刘　芳：哇，我越来越期待冬天快点儿来了。

（二）打折（Discount）

李　华：我今天去逛街了，商店里卖的衣服都很贵，而且不打折。

张丽丽：那你为什么不在淘宝上买衣服呢？

李　华：为什么在淘宝上买呢？

张丽丽：淘宝上很多店铺都打折，有的能打七折呢。

李　华：是吗？那我去看看。

张丽丽：好啊。

五 语法知识 Grammar

1. 固定句式（"越来越……"或"越……越……"）

越来越：

用法：用来比较人或事物的数量或程度随着时间的推移而不断发展或变化，是同一事物不同时期或不同条件的比较。

句型：主语＋越来越＋谓语（形容词、表示心理活动的动词）＋（了）。

例句：天气越来越冷了。

他越来越喜欢打篮球。

越……越……

用法：表示程度随情况的发展而变化。

句型：主语＋越＋谓语＋越（有时也可以加上"了"）。

例句：这本书我越看越喜欢。

我们越学越有自信了。

2. **离合词（如打折、游泳、帮忙）**

用法：是一种特殊的词，可以拆分开添加成分。

例句：今天商场里蔬菜打八折。

明天我想去游个泳。

他常常帮我的忙。

课后练习 Exercises

1. 写一写(Writing)

根据拼音写汉字。

Write down the corresponding characters according to pinyin.

ā	qū	wēi	dàn	yíng	jì	ruò
___姨	弯___	___笑	一___	___业	经___	___点

2. 连一连(Matching)

把右列的汉字与左列的汉字相连组词。

Match characters in the right column with one in the left column to form a phrase.

搀　　　　　　　惠

优　　　　　　　切

武　　　　　　　可

密　　　　　　　器

女　　　　　　　扶

宁　　　　　　　士

3. 填一填(Blank-filling)

用课文中的汉字填空。

Fill the following blanks with characters in the text.

(1) 任何时刻,我们都要学会_____笑。

(2) 这家餐厅_____业到很晚。

(3) 我的奶奶年纪大了,走路时需要有人搀_____。

(4) 即使分开了,我们也要保持_____切的联系。

4. 默一默(Writing from memory)

根据课文内容填空。

Fill in the blanks according to the text.

奄宅_____阜,_____旦孰_____。

桓公匡合,_____弱_____倾。

5. 说一说(Talking)

根据所给场景,编写对话并练习。

Based on the given situations, make dialogues and practice.

在你的生命中,你曾经遇到过对自己有重要影响的人吗？举例说说。

_____

_____

七 延伸学习 Extended reading

姜太公钓鱼

姜（Jiāng）太公,字子牙,是中国古代（gǔ dài）一位影响深远的军事（jūn shì）家和政治（zhèng zhì）家。大约3000年前,姜太公住在渭（wèi）水北岸（àn）,年过七十的他听闻（wén）西伯（bó）姬昌（Jī Chāng）招纳贤（nà xián）才,他便去投（tóu）奔姬昌。此后,他每日在渭水河边钓鱼,而且钓法十分奇特。短竿长线,线系直钩,不用诱饵（yòu ěr）。他的奇特钓（diào）鱼方法（fāng fǎ）终于（zhōng yú）传到姬昌那里。姬昌亲自带着厚（hòu）礼聘请他。太公见他诚心诚意,便答应（dā ying）为他效力。后来（hòu lái）,姜太公辅佐（fǔ zuǒ）文王,兴邦立国，还帮助文王的儿子武王姬发灭掉商朝，建立了周朝。成语"姜太公钓鱼，愿者上钩"比喻心甘情愿地上别人的圈套或是做事不计后果。

  Jiang Taigong whose literary name is Ziya, a renowned statesman and strategist in Chinese history, lived by the Weishui River about 3000 years ago. When he learned that Ji Chang was very ambitious, even though he was more than 70 years old then, he immediately wanted to get Ji's attention and help him. After that, he often went fishing by the Weishui River, but his fishing method was unusually absurd. He hung a straight fishhook without baits. Soon his weird fishing was reported to Ji Chang and Ji brought many generous gifts to invite Jiang to support him. Moved by his sincerity, Jiang decided to work for him. Jiang helped Ji Chang and his son Ji Fa overthrow the Shang Dynasty and establish the Zhou Dynasty. Later, Jiang was granted the title of Taigong, so people called him Jiang Taigong. Today, the idiomatic expression that "There are always fish willing to be caught by angler Jiang Taigong" is often used to describe someone who is willingly to fall into a trap or does something recklessly.

第十五课　晋楚更霸

Lesson Fifteen　Jin Superseding Chu

1. 描红并注音(Trace strokes and add pinyin)

2. 话题导入(Topic introduction)

你知道哪些中国古代思想家、政治家？

What ancient Chinese thinkers and politicians do you know?

| Jìn | Chǔ | gēng | bà | Zhào | Wèi | kùn | héng① |
| 晋 | 楚 | 更 | 霸 | ，赵 | 魏 | 困 | 横 |

| Jiǎ | tú | miè | Guó② | jiàn | tǔ | huì | méng |
| 假 | 途 | 灭 | 虢 | ，践 | 土 | 会 | 盟 |

| Hé③ | zūn | yuē④ | fǎ | Hán⑤ | bì | fán | xíng⑥ |
| 何 | 遵 | 约 | 法 | ，韩 | 弊 | 烦 | 刑 |

| Qǐ | Jiǎn | Pō | Mù⑦ | yòng | jūn | zuì | jīng |
| 起 | 翦 | 颇 | 牧 | ，用 | 军 | 最 | 精 |

| Xuān | wēi | shā | mò | chí | yù | dān | qīng⑧ |
| 宣 | 威 | 沙 | 漠 | ，驰 | 誉 | 丹 | 青 |

1. 注释(Notes)

①横：指"连横"，是战国时期张仪为瓦解六国联盟提出的一种外交策略（"Lianheng", a diplomatic strategy proposed by Zhang Yi during the Warring States Period to break up the alliance of the six states）。

②假途灭虢：指晋国向虞国借路去灭虢，晋灭虢后，在归途中又灭了虞国；后指以向对方借路为名义而行消灭对方的计谋(Jin borrowed a road from Yu to destroy Guo, and after Jin destroyed Guo, it destroyed Yu on the way back; later, it refers to destroying the other side in the name of borrowing a road)。

③何：萧何，西汉宰相(Xiao He, prime minister of the Western Han Dynasty)。

④约：简约的(concise)。

⑤韩：韩非，法家代表(Han Fei, the representative of Legalists)。

⑥烦刑：苛刻的刑法(harsh criminal law)。

⑦起翦颇牧：四位战国时期的将军，分别指白起、王翦、廉颇和李牧(four generals in the Warring States Period: Bai Qi, Wang Jian, Lian Po and Li Mu respectively)。

⑧丹青：作画用的颜色，此处指载入史册(originally a color used for painting; here it refers to be recorded in history books)。

2. 原文大意(Paraphrase)

晋文公、楚庄王先后成为霸主，赵国、魏国受困于张仪的连横策略。

晋国通过向虞国借路,先后消灭了虢国和虞国,晋文公在践土召集诸侯歃血会盟。

萧何遵循汉高祖简约的法律,韩非惨死于自己主张的苛刑。

秦将白起、王翦,赵将廉颇、李牧,最精通用兵作战。

他们的声誉和威望传到北方沙漠,美好的名声被永远记载在史册上。

三 汉字学习 Chinese character

| 困 | 丨 冂 円 用 困 困 |

拼音	kùn
词性	动词(v.);形容词(adj.)
释义	疲倦(tired);穷苦艰难(poor and difficult)
搭配	贫困(poverty);困难(trouble, difficulty)
例句	慈善机构向生活贫困的人群实施救济。 Charities provide relief to people living in poverty. 他有困难的时候会主动找别人倾诉。 He will reach out to others when he is in trouble.

| 途 | 丿 人 へ 全 全 刍 余 余 涂 途 |

拼音	tú
词性	名词(n.)
释义	道路(road)
搭配	前途(prospects)
例句	他对自己的前途和工作有些担心。 He is a little worried about his future and his job.

| 土 | 一 十 土 |

拼音	tǔ
词性	名词(n.);形容词(adj.)
释义	泥(mud);本地的(local)
搭配	土地(land);土豆(potatoes)

| 例句 | 中国是一片充满了神秘色彩的土地。China is a land of mystery.
我终于把土豆卖完了。
I finally sold out all the potatoes. |

何

拼音	hé
词性	名词(*n.*);代词(*pron.*)
释义	姓(family name);什么(what)
搭配	任何(any)
例句	我认为任何事情都有积极的一面。 I think there is a positive side to anything.

遵

拼音	zūn
词性	动词(*v.*)
释义	依照(according to)
搭配	遵守(abide by, observe);遵循(follow)
例句	人人都必须遵守社会公德。 Everyone must abide by social ethics. 王老师遵循自己立下的准则。 Ms. Wang follows the guidelines she has set for herself.

约

拼音	yuē
词性	动词(*adj.*)
释义	简单(simple)
搭配	节约(conserve)

| 例句 | 节约用水,保护水资源。Conserve water and protect water resources. |

烦

拼音	fán
词性	形容词(adj.)
释义	苦闷急躁(depressed and irritable)
搭配	麻烦(trouble)
例句	我们最近遇到的麻烦已经过去了。 The troubles we have had recently are behind us.

军

拼音	jūn
词性	名词(n.)
释义	兵(soldier);武装部队(armed force)
搭配	冠军(champion, championship)
例句	他的梦想是赢得一次冠军。 His dream is to win a championship.

精

拼音	jīng
词性	动词(v.)
释义	对某事擅长(be good at something)
搭配	精通(proficient)
例句	刘女士精通英文、德文。 Ms. Liu is proficient in English and German.

宣

拼音	xuān
词性	动词(v.)
释义	公开说出来(speak openly);传播(spread)
搭配	宣布(announce);宣传(disseminate)
例句	他宣布全公司放假一个月。 He announced a company-wide holiday for one month. 广告是常用的宣传方式。 Advertising is a common method of promotion.

沙

拼音	shā
词性	名词(n.);形容词(adj.)
释义	细碎的石子(finely crushed stones);干涩(dry)
搭配	沙漠(desert);沙发(sofa)
例句	没有水,怎么越过沙漠呢? How can you cross the desert without water? 一家人在沙发上坐着。The family are seated on the sofa.

漠

拼音	mò
词性	名词(n.);形容词(adj.)
释义	沙地(sand);冷淡的(indifferent)
搭配	沙漠(desert);冷漠(indifferent)
例句	塔克拉玛干沙漠是中国最大的沙漠。 The Taklimakan Desert is the largest desert in China.

（一）过关(Pass a game level)

李　华：丽丽，你知道游戏沙漠这一关怎么玩吗？

张丽丽：我知道，沙漠这一关我玩得很好。

李　华：那你教一教我。哎，我玩得不好，总是没办法过关。

张丽丽：你花太多的钱在道具上了，钱用得越快，你越出不去。

李　华：哦，我知道了。下次你带我一起玩吧。

张丽丽：好呀，下次我约你。

（二）问问题(Ask questions)

刘　芳：我知道你的成绩好得很，我有一道题目想问你。

陈士杰：过奖了。

刘　芳：你看我这道题目做得对吗？

陈士杰：我看一下。……很抱歉，你做错了。

刘　芳：我不知道怎么做。你能帮我讲解一下吗？

陈士杰：我们一起去请教老师吧。

刘　芳：好啊，好主意。

千字文

五、语法知识 Grammar

1. 结构助词(得)

   用法：补语的标志，一般用在补语前面、谓语后面。"得"后面的词语一般用来补充说明"得"前面的动作怎么样。

   句型：肯定—动词＋得＋形容词/否定—动词＋得＋不＋形容词。

   例句：这件事你做得对。

   　　　这件事你做得不对。

2. 程度补语(得)

   用法：由在形容词或表示心理活动的动词与补语之间加上"得"构成，表示动作达到某种程度。

   句型：动词/形容词＋得＋很/多/不得了。

   例句：他的成绩好得很。

   　　　她骑车急得很。

六、课后练习 Exercises

1. 写一写(Writing)

根据拼音写汉字。

Write down the corresponding characters according to pinyin.

shā	jūn	jīng	xuān
＿＿漠	冠＿＿	＿＿通	＿＿布

2. 连一连(Matching)

把右列的汉字与左列的汉字相连组词。

Match characters in the right column with one in the left column to form a phrase.

任　　　　　　　　约
困　　　　　　　　烦
遵　　　　　　　　何
沙　　　　　　　　难
麻　　　　　　　　漠
节　　　　　　　　守

3. 填一填(Blank-filling)

用本课学习的汉字填空。
Fill the following blanks with characters in the text.

(1) 我们要节_____用水,保护水资源。
(2) 中国是一片充满了神秘色彩的_____地。
(3) 刘女士_____通英文和德文。
(4) 他的梦想是赢得一次冠_____。
(5) 人人都必须_____守社会公德。
(6) 他有_____难的时候会主动找别人倾诉。

4. 标一标(Marking)

给下面的词组标注拼音。
Mark the following phrases in pinyin.

_____   _____   _____
前途   土地   麻烦

5. 说一说(Talking)

根据所给场景,编写对话并练习。
Based on the given situations, make dialogues and practice.

请说一说你玩过最有趣的游戏是什么?你玩得怎么样?

....

....

七 延伸学习 Extended reading

春秋战国

　　春秋战国(前770—前221)是中国历史上的一段分裂时期,分为春秋和战国两个时期。春秋时期,简称"春秋",指公元前770年到公元前476年,是属于东周(前770—前256)的一个时期。春秋和战国的分水岭(lǐng)是在公元前453年,晋(Jìn)国被韩(Hán)、赵(Zhào)、魏(Wèi)三个家族瓜分。战国时期简称"战国",指公元前475年到公元前221年,是中国历史上东周后期到秦(Qín)(前221—前206)统一之前的一个时期。"战国"一名取自西汉(前206—25)刘向(前77—前6)所编订的《战国策》。

The Spring and Autumn Period and the Warring States Period were two divided periods in the history of China. The Spring and Autumn Period refers to the period from 770 B.C. to 476 B.C., which was a period of the Eastern Zhou Dynasty(770 B.C. - 256 B.C.). The dividing line between the Spring and Autumn Period and the Warring States Period was the year 453 B.C. when the State of Jin was divided by the three clans of Han, Zhao and Wei. The Warring States Period refers to the period from 475 B.C. to 221 B.C., which was another period of the Eastern Zhou Dynasty before the reunification of China by the Qin Dynasty(221 B.C. - 206 B.C.). The name of the Warring States Period is taken from the *Records of the Warring States Period* compiled and edited by Liu Xiang(77 B.C. - 6 B.C.) in the Western Han Dynasty(206 B.C. - A.D. 25).

第十六课　九州禹迹

Lesson Sixteen　Footprints of Dayu in Ancient China

1. 描红并注音(Trace strokes and add pinyin)

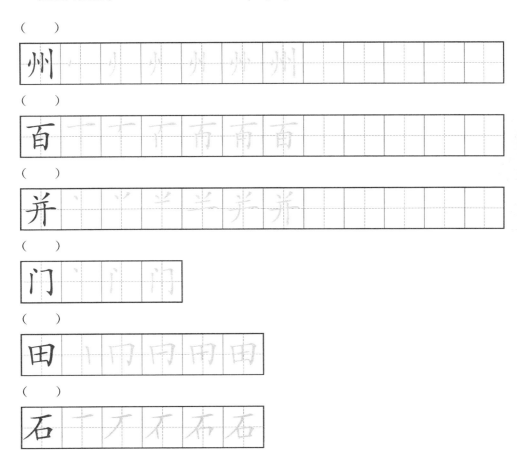

2. 话题导入(Topic introduction)

你去过中国哪些有名的景点？
What famous scenic spots in China have you been to?

一 学习原文 Text

千字文

Jiǔ	zhōu①	Yǔ	jì	bǎi	jùn	Qín	bìng
九	州	禹	迹	， 百	郡	秦	并 。

Yuè	zōng	Tài	dài②	shàn	zhǔ	Yún	Tíng③
岳	宗	泰	岱	， 禅	主	云	亭 。

Yàn	mén	zǐ	sài④	Jī	Tián	Chì	Chéng⑤
雁	门	紫	塞	， 鸡	田	赤	城 。

Kūn	chí	jié	shí	Jù	Yě	Dòng	Tíng
昆	池	碣	石	， 巨	野	洞	庭 。

Kuàng	yuǎn	mián	miǎo⑥	yán	xiù	yǎo	míng⑦
旷	远	绵	邈	， 岩	岫	杳	冥 。

1. 注释(Notes)

①九州：中国古代分冀、豫、雍、扬、兖、徐、梁、青、荆九州。后"九州"泛指中国或天下(China)。

②岳：指五岳，即东岳泰山、西岳华山、南岳衡山、北岳恒山、中岳嵩山(the Five Great Mountains of China)。宗：尊崇(reverent)。泰岱：泰山(Mount Tai)。

③禅：在泰山下祭祀土地曰"禅"(offering sacrifices to the Land God at the foot of Mount Tai)。云亭：泰山脚下的云山和亭山(Yunshan and Tingshan at the foot of Mount Tai)。

④雁门：雁门关(Yanmen Fortress)。紫塞：北方边塞，这里指长城(the Great Wall)。

⑤鸡田：西北塞外地名(place name)。赤城：山名(name of a mountain)。

⑥绵邈：连绵遥远的样子(long and distant)。

⑦岫：山洞(cave)；杳冥：昏暗幽深(dim and deep)。

2. 原文大意(Paraphrase)

九州大地遍布大禹治水的足迹，秦朝吞并六国，统一全国各郡。
五岳以泰山为尊，历代帝王都在云山和亭山主持禅礼。
名关有雁门关，要塞有万里长城；驿站有鸡田，奇山有赤城。
昆明的滇池，河北的碣石，山东的巨野，湖南的洞庭湖，都是风景胜地。
中国土地辽阔遥远，无边无际；名山奇谷幽深秀丽，气象万千。

三 汉字学习 Chinese character

并

拼音	bìng
词性	动词(v.)
释义	合在一起(put them together)
搭配	合并(merge)
例句	这两所学校合并已经一年了。 It has been a year since the two schools merged.

城

拼音	chéng
词性	名词(n.)
释义	都市(city)；围绕都市的高墙(high city walls)
搭配	城市(city)
例句	晚饭后，我绕着这座城市溜达了一圈。 After dinner, I took a stroll around the city.

石

拼音	shí
词性	名词(n.)
释义	一种矿物质(stone; rock)
搭配	石头(stone)；岩石(rock)
例句	他们被石头砸伤了。They were injured by stones.

紫

拼音	zǐ
词性	形容词(adj.)
释义	红和蓝合成的颜色(purple; violet)
搭配	紫色(purple; violet)
例句	她穿着紫色和绿色的丝绸。 She wore purple and green silk.

池

拼音	chí
词性	名词(n.)
释义	水塘(pool; pond)
搭配	池塘(pond)
例句	池塘里有一些鱼。There are some fish in the pond.

洞

拼音	dòng
词性	名词(n.)
释义	窟窿,深穴(hole, cavity)
搭配	洞穴(cave)
例句	那些洞穴深约20公里。 The caves extend for about 20 kilometers.

四 日常对话 Dialogue

(一) 偶遇并问候(Encounter and greet each other)

Zhāng Lì li　　Nǐ hǎo, hǎo jiǔ bú jiàn a
张　丽丽:你好,好久不见啊!

Lǐ　Huá　Shì a, hǎo jiǔ bú jiàn. Nǐ zuì jìn máng ma
李　华:是啊,好久不见。你最近忙吗?

Zhāng Lì li　Hěn máng
张　丽丽:很忙。

李 华：你在忙什么呢？

张丽丽：我忙着写论文。

李 华：你父母的身体还好吗？

张丽丽：很好，谢谢你的关心。

李 华：现在你去哪儿？

张丽丽：我去超市买东西。你呢？

李 华：我去校园逛逛。

张丽丽：好的，那下次再聊，再见！

李 华：好的，再见！

（二）课表（Timetable）

李 华：丽丽，今天星期几？

张丽丽：星期五。

李 华：今天我们有课吗？上午还是下午？

张丽丽：今天上午有汉语口语课，下午没有课。

李 华：我们在哪里上课？

张丽丽：在二楼二零五教室。

李 华：谢谢。

张丽丽：不客气。

李 华：等会儿我们一起走吧。

张丽丽：好啊。

五 语法知识 Grammar

可能补语

（1）用法：表示可能性，表示动词或形容词可能或者不可能有某种结果或趋向。

句型：动词/形容词＋得/不得。

例句：这件衣服晒不晒得？

　　　这次考试很重要，马虎不得。

（2）用法：用在动词和形容词后面，补充说明能不能、可以不可以的成分。

句型：动词＋得了/不了。

例句：这个菜有点辣，你吃得了吗？

　　　菜太多了，咱们吃不了。

 六 课后练习 Exercises

1. 写一写(Writing)

根据拼音写汉字。

Write down the corresponding characters according to pinyin.

dòng	zǐ	chéng	bìng
＿＿穴	＿＿色	＿＿市	合＿＿

2. 连一连(Matching)

把右列的汉字与左列的汉字相连组词。

Match characters in the right column with one in the left column to form a phrase.

池　　　　　　　　穴
紫　　　　　　　　头
石　　　　　　　　塘
洞　　　　　　　　远
遥　　　　　　　　市
城　　　　　　　　色

3. 填一填(Blank-filling)

用适当的汉字填空。

Fill the following blanks with proper characters.

(1) 这个_____市景色秀丽，非常适合居住。

(2) 我搬不动这块_____头。

(3) _____塘里有一群鸭子在游泳。

(4) 姐姐穿着_____色的裙子。

(5) 到了冬天，动物都躲到_____穴中了。

(6) 这两所学校在三年前合_____了。

4. 默一默(Writing from memory)

根据课文内容填空。

Fill in the blanks according to the text.

_____州禹迹，_____郡秦_____。

岳宗泰岱，禅_____ _____亭。

雁_____ _____塞，_____田赤_____。

昆_____碣石，巨野_____ _____。

旷_____绵邈，岩岫杳冥。

5. 说一说(Talking)

根据所给场景，编写对话并练习。

Based on the given situations, make dialogues and practice.

询问自己的同学上课内容是否能听懂。

提示：可能补语。

七 延伸学习 Extended reading

五 岳

五岳是中国五大名山的总称，是远古山神崇拜、五行观念和帝王封禅相结合的产物，以中原为中心，按东、西、南、北、中方位命名。五

千字文

岳分别是中岳嵩(sōng)山、东岳泰(tài)山、西岳华山、南岳衡(héng)山、北岳恒(héng)山。五岳各具特色：东岳泰山之雄(zhī xióng)，西岳华山之险(xiǎn)，南岳衡山之秀(xiù)，北岳恒山之奇，中岳嵩山之峻(jùn)，早已闻名于世界。

  The Five Great Mountains is used to refer to five famous mountains collectively in China. They are the products of the combination of the ancient mountain god worship, the concept of Wuxing(Five Elements, i. e. metal, wood, water, fire and earth) and the imperial worship of Heaven and Earth. With the Central Plain as the center, the five great mountains are named according to their locations—East, West, South, North, and Center. They are Mount Song in the center, Mount Tai in the east, Mount Hua in the west, Mount Heng(衡) in the south and Mount Heng(恒) in the north. These five great mountains have their unique characteristics: Mount Tai is majestic, Mount Hua is perilous, Mount Heng(衡) is beautiful, Mount Heng(恒) is peculiar and Mount Song is steep. They have long been well-known to the world.

第十七课　治本于农

Lesson Seventeen　Agriculture, Foundation of a Country

1. 描红并注音(Trace strokes and add pinyin)

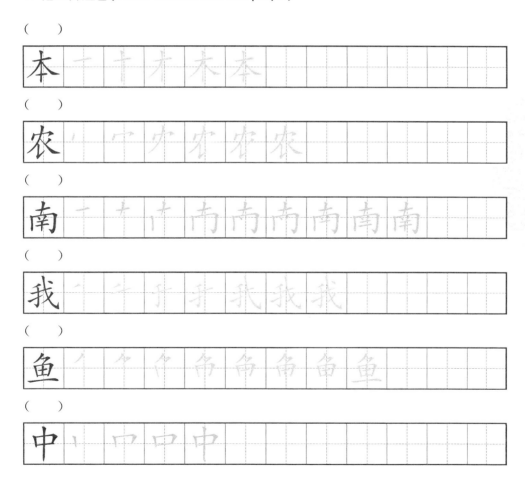

2. 话题导入(Topic introduction)

谈谈你国家的农业发展情况。

Talk about the development of agriculture in your country.

Zhì	běn	yú	nóng		wù	zī	jià	sè①	
治	本	于	农	，	务	兹	稼	穑	。
Chù②	zǎi③	nán	mǔ		wǒ	yì	shǔ	jì	
俶	载	南	亩	，	我	艺	黍	稷	。
Shuì	shú	gòng	xīn		quàn	shǎng	chù④	zhì⑤	
税	熟	贡	新	，	劝	赏	黜	陟	。
Mèng	Kē	dūn	sù		Shǐ	Yú	bǐng	zhí	
孟	轲	敦	素	，	史	鱼	秉	直	。
Shù	jī⑥	zhōng	yōng		láo	qiān	jǐn	chì	
庶	几	中	庸	，	劳	谦	谨	敕	。

1. 注释(Notes)

①稼穑:种植和收割,泛指农业活动(planting and harvesting, generally referring to agricultural activities)。

②俶:开始(start)。

③载:从事(engage in)。

④黜:降职(demote)。

⑤陟:上升职位(promotion)。

⑥庶几:差不多(almost)。

2. 原文大意(Paraphrase)

农业是治理国家的根本,一定要做好种植和收割。

播种的时候,种上五谷作物。收获的季节,农民用成熟的庄稼交纳税粮,种好种坏赏罚分明。

孟子朴素敦厚,史鱼禀性刚直。

做人要尽量不偏不倚,并且勤劳、谦逊、谨慎、端正,严于律己。

农

拼音	nóng
词性	名词(n.)
释义	种庄稼(crop)
搭配	农业(agriculture)
例句	中国是农业大国。 China is a great agricultural country.

拼音	zhì
词性	动词(v.)
释义	管理(manage);处理(handle)
搭配	治疗(treatment)
例句	经过医生的治疗,他的病好了。 After the doctor's treatment, he recovered from his illness.

拼音	yì
词性	名词(n.)
释义	才能(talent)
搭配	艺术(art)
例句	音乐和绘画都是艺术。 Music and painting are both arts.

拼音	zǎi
词性	动词(v.)
释义	记录(record);描绘(depict)
搭配	下载(download)

续表

| 例句 | 我习惯在网上下载免费软件。
I am used to downloading free software online. |

赏

拼音	shǎng
词性	动词(v.)
释义	赠送,奖励(reward);因爱好某种东西而观看(enjoy;appreciate)
搭配	欣赏(appreciate;enjoy)
例句	我们要学会欣赏别人。 We must learn to appreciate others.

劝

拼音	quàn
词性	动词(v.)
释义	说服(convince)
搭配	劝说(persuade)
例句	王明劝说我要好好学习。 Wang Ming persuaded me to study hard.

史

拼音	shǐ
词性	名词(n.)
释义	姓(family name);自然界和人类社会的发展过程(development process of nature and human society)
搭配	历史(history)
例句	中国有悠久的历史。China has a long history.

劳

拼音	láo
词性	形容词(adj.)
释义	辛苦,辛勤(hard-working)
搭配	劳动(labor)
例句	我们都要热爱劳动。We all love labor.

第十七课　治本于农

四 日常对话 Dialogue

(一) 农家乐 (Agritainment)

刘芳：我们明天约李华他们一起去农家乐吧。

陈士杰：不是约好后天吗?

刘芳：对不起,我记错了,幸亏问了你一下。

陈士杰：那家农家乐怎么样?

刘芳：离学校不远,开车大概半小时。农家乐设计得很好。我在网上查了一下,食物都是当天的,还有一些特色菜,但是如果去那里,需要我们打电话提前预约。

陈士杰：听上去很不错。

刘芳：对,是个休闲的好去处。

(二) 运动 (Sports)

刘芳：你周末一般做什么运动?

陈士杰：我一般打篮球,你呢?

Liú Fāng Wǒ xǐ huan yú jiā
刘 芳：我 喜 欢 瑜 伽。

Chén Shì jié Nǐ yì bān dōu zài nǎ lǐ zuò yú jiā jiàn shēn fáng ma
陈 士 杰：你 一 般 都 在 哪 里 做 瑜 伽，健 身 房 吗？

Liú Fāng Duì a nà lǐ yǒu zhuān yè de lǎo shī zhǐ dǎo
刘 芳：对 啊，那 里 有 专 业 的 老 师 指 导。

Chén Shì jié Nǎ ge jiàn shēn fáng
陈 士 杰：哪 个 健 身 房？

Liú Fāng Xué xiào páng biān de nà ge
刘 芳：学 校 旁 边 的 那 个。

Chén Shì jié Nà ge hěn bú cuò wǒ jīng cháng qù
陈 士 杰：那 个 很 不 错，我 经 常 去。

1. 数量补语

用法：补语之一，表示动作发生的次数，动作持续的时间或者动作实现以后到目前所经历的整段时间。

句型：动词＋数量补语。

例句：你把书再读两遍。

这个月他来过几次。

2. 反问句（不是……吗？）

用法：表示强调，加强语气。

句型：不是……吗？

例句：这不是你说的吗？

他不是去北京了吗？

家乡的风景不是很美吗？

1. 写一写（Writing）

根据拼音写汉字。

Write down the corresponding characters according to pinyin.

yì ____术   shǐ 历____   zǎi 下____

láo	zhì	nóng
＿＿动	＿＿疗	＿＿民

2. 连一连(Matching)

把右列的汉字与左列的汉字相连组词。

Match characters in the right column with one in the left column to form a phrase.

劳	史
农	说
欣	业
劝	动
历	赏

3. 填一填(Blank-filling)

用课文中的汉字填空。

Fill the following blanks with characters in the text.

(1) 他热爱＿＿＿＿动,老师都喜欢他。

(2) 我经常从网上下＿＿＿＿学习资料。

(3) 我爸爸是＿＿＿＿民,他在山上种了很多菜。

4. 标一标(Marking)

给下面的词组标注拼音。

Mark the following phrases in pinyin.

＿＿＿＿	＿＿＿＿	＿＿＿＿
劝说	植树	沉默

5. 说一说(Talking)

根据所给场景,编写对话并练习。

Based on the given situations, make dialogues and practice.

你知道中国都有哪些主要的农产品吗?

提示:大米、小麦、玉米、黄豆……

＿＿

＿＿

＿＿

千字文

袁 隆 平

袁隆平(1930—2021)，出生于北京。1953年毕业后，他一直从事农业教育及杂交水稻研究。1995年，袁隆平被选为中国工程院院士，并成功研制出两系法杂交水稻。他在1997年提出超级杂交稻育种技术路线，在2000年实现了农业部制定的中国超级稻育种的第一期目标，在2004年提前一年实现了超级稻第二期目标。袁隆平是世界著名的杂交水稻专家，是我国杂交水稻研究领域的开创者和带头人。他在2006年4月当选美国科学院外籍院士，被誉为"杂交水稻之父"。袁隆平说过自己有两个梦——"禾下乘凉梦"和"杂交水稻覆盖全球梦"。正是这份信念，让他一直坚持利用科学解决全世界的吃饭问题。

Yuan Longping(1930-2021), born in Beijing, has been engaged in agricultural education and hybrid rice research since his graduation in 1953. In 1995, he was selected as a member of the Chinese Academy of Engineering and developed Two-line Hybrid Rice. In 1997, he proposed the super hybrid breeding technology route. The first phase of China's super grain breeding target set by the Ministry of Agriculture was achieved by him in 2000; and the second phase of super grain was achieved one year ahead of schedule in 2004. He is a world-renowned expert on hybrid rice, a pioneer and leader in the field of hybrid rice research in China. In April 2006, he was elected a foreign fellow of the American Academy of Sciences and was known as the "Father of Hybrid Rice". He said he had two dreams—"enjoying the cool under the shade of the crops" and "hybrid rice covering the globe". It was this belief that led him to insist on solving worldwide food problems with science.

第十八课　聆音察理

Lesson Eighteen　Hearing the Sound and Telling the Truth

 课前练习 Warm-up

1. 描红并注音(Trace strokes and add pinyin)

( )
| 聆 | 一 | ㄏ | ㄐ | 耳 | 耳 | 耳 | 耶 | 聆 | 聆 | 聆 | 聆 |

( )
| 音 | 一 | 亠 | 立 | 立 | 产 | 产 | 音 | 音 | 音 | | |

( )
| 林 | 一 | 十 | 才 | 木 | 木 | 朴 | 朴 | 林 | | | |

( )
| 两 | 一 | 厂 | 厂 | 丙 | 丙 | 两 | 两 | | | | |

( )
| 见 | 丨 | 冂 | 贝 | 见 | | | | | | | |

( )
| 闲 | 丶 | 丿 | 门 | 闫 | 闲 | 闲 | 闲 | | | | |

2. 话题导入(Topic introduction)

你从中国古人身上学会了哪些道理？请详述。

What morals have you learned from ancient Chinese people? please elaborate your answer.

一、学习原文 Text

聆 yīn chá lǐ，jiàn mào biàn sè。
聆 音 察 理 , 鉴 貌 辨 色 。

Yí jué① jiā yóu②，miǎn qí zhī zhí③。
贻 厥 嘉 猷 , 勉 其 祗 植 。

Xǐng gōng jī jiè，chǒng zēng kàng jí。
省 躬 讥 诫 , 宠 增 抗 极 。

Dài rǔ jìn chǐ，lín gāo④ xìng jí。
殆 辱 近 耻 , 林 皋 幸 即 。

Liǎng Shū⑤ jiàn jī，jiě zǔ shuí bī。
两 疏 见 机 , 解 组 谁 逼 。

Suǒ jū xián chǔ，chén mò jì liáo。
索 居 闲 处 , 沉 默 寂 寥 。

1. 注释(Notes)

①贻：留下(remain)。厥：他的(his)。

②猷：计划(plan)。

③祗：恭敬(respect)。植：立身于不败之地(in an invincible position)。

④皋：水边的高地(highlands by the water)。

⑤两疏：汉代疏广、疏受叔侄[Shu Guang(uncle) and Shu Shou(nephew) in the Han Dynasty]。

2. 原文大意(Paraphrase)

听人说话要思考其中的道理，看人面貌要猜出他的心情。

给人正确高明的忠告或建议，鼓励别人谨慎小心地做事。

听到别人的讥刺劝告，要反省自身；备受恩宠也不要得意忘形，对抗权尊。

如果知道有危险侮辱的事将要发生，应该远离，才可以幸免于祸。

汉代疏广和疏受叔侄在合适的时间远离，有谁逼迫他们辞去官职呢？

离开皇帝独自居住，整天不用多说话，自己安静地生活是一件好事。

三 汉字学习 Chinese character

察

拼音	chá
词性	动词(v.)
释义	仔细看(observe carefully);调查研究(research)
搭配	观察(observe)
例句	你如果仔细观察就可能有新发现。If you observe carefully, you may make new discoveries.

貌

拼音	mào
词性	名词(n.)
释义	面容,外表的样子(appearance)
搭配	礼貌(politeness)
例句	礼貌对每个人都很重要。Politeness is very important to everyone.

拼音	zhí
词性	动词(v.);名词(n.)

续表

释义	种(plant)；谷类、花草、树木的称呼(general term for crops, flowers and trees)
搭配	植物(plant)
例句	我最喜欢的植物是仙人掌。My favorite plant is cactuses.

增

拼音	zēng
词性	动词(v.)
释义	加多(increase)
搭配	增长(increase)
例句	今年参加比赛的人数增长了。 The number of participants has increased this year.

极

拼音	jí
词性	形容词(adj.)
释义	最终的(ultimate)
搭配	积极(active)
例句	王明上课积极回答问题。 Wang Ming actively answers questions in class.

幸

拼音	xìng
词性	名词(n.)；副词(adv.)
释义	福气(blessing)；避免灾害(save someone from disasters)
搭配	幸福(happiness)；幸亏(fortunately)

例句	幸福是用勤劳和智慧创造出来的。 Happiness is created with hard work and wisdom. 幸亏有你帮我，我才能完成作业。 Thanks for your help, I can finish my homework.

即

拼音	jí
词性	动词(v.)
释义	就是(be)
搭配	即使(even if)
例句	即使雨下得再大，我也要去上学。 Even if it rains heavily, I still must go to school.

林

拼音	lín
词性	名词(n.)
释义	许多树木或竹子(trees or bamboos growing in a place)
搭配	森林(forest)
例句	那只鹿迅速跑进了森林里。The deer quickly ran into the forest.

居

拼音	jū
词性	动词(v.)；名词(n.)
释义	住(live)；住的地方(a place of residence)
搭配	邻居(neighbor)
例句	我的邻居非常友好。My neighbor is very friendly.

沉

拼音	chén
词性	形容词(adj.)
释义	程度深(deep)
搭配	沉默(silent)
例句	王明沉默了一会儿才回答这个问题。Wang Ming was silent for a while before answering this question.

默 | 丨 | 冂 | 冂 | 冂 | 四 | 甲 | 甲 | 里 | 黑 | 黑 | 黑

黑 | 黑 | 默 | 默 | 默

拼音	mò
词性	形容词(adj.)
释义	不说话(keep silent)
搭配	幽默(humor)
例句	他是个幽默的人。He is a humorous person.

四 日常对话 Dialogue

(一) 周末新书签售会 (Signing session for a new book)

Liú Fāng　Nǐ zhōu mò qù cān jiā xīn shū qiān shòu huì ma
刘　芳：你周末去参加新书签售会吗？

Chén Shì jié　Nǎ wèi zuò jiā de
陈士杰：哪位作家的？

Liú Fāng　Zhōng Guó zuò jiā Liú Cí xīn
刘　芳：中国作家刘慈欣。

Chén Shì jié　Wǒ zhī dao le　tā shì Zhōng Guó fēi cháng yǒu míng de kē huàn xiǎo
陈士杰：我知道了，他是中国非常有名的科幻小
　　　　shuō zuò jiā
　　　　说作家。

Liú Fāng　Méi cuò　Nǐ kàn guo tā shén me zuò pǐn ma
刘　芳：没错。你看过他什么作品吗？

Chén Shì jié　Wǒ kàn guo tā de sān tǐ hé liú làng dì qiú　dōu fēi cháng jīng cǎi
陈士杰：我看过他的《三体》和《流浪地球》，都非常精彩。

刘　芳:是的。你知道吗?《流浪地球》还被拍成了电影。

陈士杰:那我们参加完新书签售会,一起去看这部电影吧?

刘　芳:好啊!

(二) 端午节活动(Dragon Boat Festival Activities)

刘　芳:你这个周末去参加端午节活动吗?

陈士杰:是在学校广场举行的吗?

刘　芳:没错。

陈士杰:端午节的来历是什么?

刘　芳:为了纪念伟大的爱国主义诗人屈原。

陈士杰:端午节都有哪些活动呢?

刘　芳:有包粽子、赛龙舟等等。

陈士杰:那听起来很好玩。

刘　芳:是的,我们一起去参加吧!

陈士杰:好的。

五 语法知识 Grammar

1. 疑问代词的非疑问用法

用法:疑问代词从询问功能转移为陈述、指令等功能。

句型:疑问词＋陈述句。

例句:谁(所有人)都不明白。

　　　谁都知道他不喜欢打篮球。

　　　周末的时候,哪里都是人。

2. 关系副词(再)

用法:关系副词,兼有副词与连接词两种作用,表示重复或第二次,一般放在动词前,表示"又一次"。

句型:句子＋再＋动词。

例句:你写了作业再玩。

我考完试再去北京。

我做完这项工作再休息。

1. 写一写(Writing)

根据拼音写汉字。

Write down the corresponding characters according to pinyin.

zhí　　　　　zēng　　　　　xìng　　　　　chén
＿＿＿物　　＿＿＿长　　＿＿＿运　　＿＿＿默

2. 填一填(Blank-filling)

用适当的汉字填空。

Fill the following blanks with proper characters.

(1) 我的邻＿＿＿＿对我帮助很多。

(2) 我们一起去森＿＿＿＿玩吧?

(3) 王明是讲礼＿＿＿＿的好学生。

3. 默一默(Writing from memory)

根据课文内容填空。

Fill in the blanks according to the text.

聆＿＿＿察理,鉴貌辨＿＿＿。

贻厥嘉猷,勉其祗＿＿＿。

省躬讥诫,宠＿＿＿抗极。

殆辱＿＿＿耻,＿＿＿皋幸即。

＿＿＿疏见机,解＿＿＿谁逼。

索居＿＿＿处,＿＿＿默寂寥。

4. 连一连(Matching)

把右列的汉字与左列的汉字相连组词。
Match characters in the right column with one in the left column to form a phrase.

邻　　　　　　　　　　林
增　　　　　　　　　　树
沉　　　　　　　　　　默
植　　　　　　　　　　长
森　　　　　　　　　　居

5. 说一说(Talking)

根据所给场景,编写对话并练习。
Based on the given situations, make dialogues and practice.

请说一说你喜欢哪个古代名人？为什么？

提示:孔子、老子、庄子等

_____

_____

_____

两疏——疏广与疏受

　　疏广(？—公元前45)自幼好学,精通《春秋》,在家教学,向他求学的人中有的来自很远的地方。后来疏广被征为博士、太中大夫、太子太傅。疏广兄长的儿子疏受也因贤良被选为太子少傅。疏受崇尚礼义,谦恭谨慎,思维敏捷而善于言辞。疏广对疏受说:"我听说知足的人不蒙受羞辱,知道适可而止的人不遭遇危险,功成身退,是符合天道规律的。如今我们叔侄为官,位至二千石,可谓是功成名就了,如果现在我们不适可而止辞官离去,恐怕将来会后悔的。不如我们叔侄一起辞官,告老还乡。"当天叔侄二人都上书称病要求告老还乡。叔侄二人同时主动辞官,受到人们尊重。

Shu Guang(? -45 B.C.) was eager to learn since he was a child, proficient in *The Spring and Autumn Annals*, and teaching at home. Some people came afar to learn from him. Later, Shu Guang was recruited as a high official. Shu Shou, a son of his elder brother, was also selected as a tutor for the prince because of his virtuousness. He advocated etiquette. And he was always modest and discreet, quick-witted and eloquent. Shu Guang said to Shu Shou: "I heard that content people are not easily humiliated, and those who know where to draw the line shall not be in danger. It conforms to the law of heaven to resign when you have succeeded. Now that we have achieved a lot as officials, we should feel satisfied. If we don't resign now, we might regret in the future. Why don't we retire together and go back to our hometown to live a relaxed life?" So, they both submitted their resignations on the same day with the excuse that their health was too poor for them to continue their service and begged to be allowed to return home for convalescence. The two of them have always been respected for their contentment and voluntary resignation.

第十九课　求古寻论

Lesson Nineteen　Exploring the Ancients and Reading Some Famous Quotes

1. 描红并注音(Trace strokes and add pinyin)

2. 话题导入(Topic introduction)

当你遇到烦恼时,怎样让自己变得快乐呢?

When you are worried, how to make yourself happy?

<pre>
Qiú   gǔ   xún   lùn   sàn   lǜ   xiāo yáo
求   古   寻   论 ,   散   虑   逍   遥   。
Xīn   zòu① lèi   qiǎn   qī②   xiè   huān zhāo
欣   奏   累   遣 ,   戚   谢   欢   招   。
Qú   hé   dì   lì③   yuán mǎng④ chōu tiáo⑤
渠   荷   的   历 ,   园   莽   抽   条   。
Pí   pa⑥   wǎn   cuì   wú   tóng⑦ zǎo   diāo⑧
枇   杷   晚   翠 ,   梧   桐   蚤   凋   。
Chén gēn   wěi   yì⑨   luò   yè   piāo yáo
陈   根   委   翳 ,   落   叶   飘   摇   。
Yóu   kūn⑩ dú   yùn   líng mó   jiàng xiāo⑪
游   鹍   独   运 ,   凌   摩   绛   霄   。
</pre>

1. 注释(Notes)

①奏:会合(assemble)。

②戚:忧虑(worries)。谢:拒绝(refuse)。

③的历:光彩绚烂的样子(splendid look)。

④莽:茂盛的草(lush grass)。

⑤抽条:发芽(sprout)。

⑥枇杷:亚洲的一种常绿乔木(loquat)。

⑦梧桐:落叶乔木,树皮绿色(Chinese parasol)。

⑧蚤:早(early)。凋,草木枯萎(wither)。

⑨翳:树木枯死(trees wither or die)。

⑩鹍:古书上说的一种形似天鹅的大鸟(a swan-like bird)。

⑪霄:天空(sky)。

2. 原文大意(Paraphrase)

探求古人古事,看看至理名言;不要为过去烦恼,每天要自由快乐。

轻松的事凑到一起,费力的事丢在一边;消除不尽的烦恼,得来无限的快乐。

池塘中的荷花开得那么美丽,园林里的青草也变绿了。

到了冬天,枇杷树的叶子还是很绿;但是梧桐树一到秋天,叶子就掉了。
地面上有曲折的老树根,掉下来的树叶随着秋风到处飘动。
只有远游的鸥鸟独自翱翔,直冲布满彩霞的云霄。

汉字学习 Chinese character

古 一十十古古

拼音	gǔ
词性	名词(n.);形容词(adj.)
释义	很久以前(long long ago);旧(old)
搭配	古代(ancient);古典(classical)
例句	长城是举世闻名的古代建筑。 The Great Wall is a worldwide famous ancient building. 他喜欢古典音乐。He likes classical music.

寻 ㇇彐彐寻寻

拼音	xún
词性	动词(v.);副词(adv.)
释义	找(look for);经常(often)
搭配	寻找(look for);寻常(ordinarily)
例句	他在寻找一只小羊。He is looking for a lamb. 冬天下雪是很寻常的事。Snow in winter is very common.

散 一十卅卅井芇芇芇背背散

拼音	sàn;sǎn
词性	动词(v.);形容词(adj.)
释义	分开(separate);懒(lazy)

搭配	散步(walk);懒散(sǎn)(lazy)
例句	我们一起去散步吧。Let's take a walk together. 他是一个懒散的人。He is a lazy person.

虑

拼音	lǜ
词性	动词(v.);名词(n.)
释义	思考(think);思想(thought)
搭配	考虑(consider);多虑(overthinking)
例句	他考虑了很久。He thought about it for a long time. 你真的多虑了！You really worry too much!

欣

拼音	xīn
词性	动词(v.);形容词(adj.)
释义	高兴(glad);喜爱(love)
搭配	欣喜(delighted);欣赏(appreciate)
例句	再次相见,他们备感欣喜。 They are very delighted to see each other again. 他们正在欣赏贝多芬的交响曲。 They are appreciating Beethoven's symphony.

招

拼音	zhāo
词性	动词(v.);名词(n.)
释义	打手势叫人来(sign for someone to come);办法(way)
搭配	招聘(recruitment);妙招(great trick)

例句	前几天我还看到了KFC的招聘。 The other day I also saw the recruitment of KFC. 请教老师是学习知识的妙招。 Asking teachers is a great trick to learn knowledge.

历

拼音	lì
词性	动词(v.)
释义	体验(experience)
搭配	经历(experience)
例句	经历过苦难的人更懂得珍惜幸福。People who have experienced misery know how to cherish happiness.

抽

拼音	chōu
词性	动词(v.)
释义	从事物中提取一部分(extract a part of something)
搭配	抽烟(smoking)
例句	抽烟有害健康。Smoking is bad for your health.

根

拼音	gēn
词性	名词(n.);量词(quantifier)
释义	主干下部长在土里的部分(the lower part of the stem growing in the soil);指长条的东西(something long)
搭配	树根(tree root);一根筷子(one chopstick)
例句	用一根筷子无法吃饭。You can't eat with one chopstick.

委

千字文

拼音	wěi
词性	动词(v.)
释义	把事情交给别人办(delegate things to others)
搭配	委托(entrust, authorize)
例句	他委托我去买办公用品。 He authorized me to buy office supplies.

落 一 艹 艹 艹 艹 莎 莎 苓 落

拼音	luò
词性	动词(v.);名词(n.)
释义	往下掉(fall)
搭配	掉落(fall, drop)
例句	雪花从天空掉落到地面上。 Snowflakes fell from the sky to the ground.

叶 一 口 口 叶 叶

拼音	yè
词性	名词(n.)
释义	植物的一部分(part of a plant)
搭配	树叶(tree leave)
例句	好美的树叶！What beautiful leaves!

摇 一 寸 扌 扌 扌 护 护 护 挥 挥

摇 摇

| 拼音 | yáo |

词性	动词(v.)
释义	摆动(swing)
搭配	摇头(shake one's head);摇动(shake)
例句	他用力摇晃着我的手,显得很激动。He shakes my hand forcefully to show his excitement. 小明在摇动一个玻璃瓶。Xiaoming is shaking a glass bottle.

独

拼音	dú
词性	形容词(adj.);动词(v.)
释义	单一(single)
搭配	单独(alone)
例句	老虎喜欢单独行动。Tigers like acting alone.

摩

拼音	mó
词性	动词(v.)
释义	摩擦(friction)
搭配	按摩(massage)
例句	她正在给妈妈按摩呢。She's giving her mother a massage.

四 日常对话 Dialogue

(一) 找资料 (Look for references)

李华:你看,花园里的植物都发芽了,春天来了。

张丽丽：哎，我现在没有心情。

李华：你怎么了？

张丽丽：昨天历史老师给了一个问题让我们讨论，还布置了作业，我现在一点儿办法都没有。

李华：你去图书馆找资料吗？

张丽丽：去了，图书馆里历史方面的书我几乎全找了，还是不够。

李华：即使图书馆里没有，你也可以上网找啊。

张丽丽：我正在找呢，但是网上的资料很多，我需要整理一下。

李华：加油吧！

(二) 找钥匙 (Look for the key)

李华：外面下着雪，刘芳在操场上做什么？

张丽丽：她正在找钥匙呢！

李华：一会儿就要上课了，她一个人找很难找到，要不我们一起去帮帮她吧！

张丽丽：好呀。

李华：嗯。我们去那边看看！快看！那不是刘芳的钥匙吗？

张丽丽：在哪儿呀？我怎么没有看见？

李华：在那儿！在那片树叶旁边。

张丽丽：刘芳！快过来，你的钥匙在这儿呢！

（ Zhāng Lì li xiàng Liú Fāng zhāo shǒu。Liú Fāng jí máng pǎo guo lai，kàn dào
张 丽 丽 向 刘 芳 招 手。刘 芳 急 忙 跑 过 来，看 到
Zhāng Lì li shǒu lǐ de yào shi xīn xǐ de xiào le
张 丽 丽 手 里 的 钥 匙 欣 喜 地 笑 了。）

Liú Fāng：Xiè xie nǐ men！Wǒ jī hū zhǎo biàn le zhěng gè cāo chǎng dōu méi
刘 芳：谢 谢 你 们！我 几 乎 找 遍 了 整 个 操 场 都 没
kàn dào wǒ de yào shi，hái shì nǐ men lì hai
看 到 我 的 钥 匙，还 是 你 们 厉 害！

Zhāng Lì li：Bú kè qi，zhǐ yǒu shí fēn zhōng jiù yào shàng kè le，wǒ men gǎn
张 丽 丽：不 客 气，只 有 十 分 钟 就 要 上 课 了，我 们 赶
kuài guò qu
快 过 去。

1. 固定句式(假设让步：即使……也)

用法：假设复句，前一个分句假设某种情况，后一个分句说出结果。两个分句是条件
　　　与结果的关系。

句型：即使……，也……。

例句：即使明天下雨，我们也要去参加足球比赛。
　　　即使你去，我也不去。

2. 程度副词(几乎)

用法：指差一点，差不多，接近。

句型：主语＋几乎＋……。

例句：中国的大城市我几乎都去过。
　　　我几乎每年回一次北京。

1. 写一写(Writing)

根据拼音写汉字。

Write down the corresponding characters according to pinyin.

　　yuán　　　　　　　　lùn　　　　　　　　yè
花＿＿＿　　　　　言＿＿＿　　　　　树＿＿＿

2. 连一连(Matching)

把右列的汉字与左列的汉字相连组词。

Match characters in the right column with one in the left column to form a phrase.

逍　　　　　　　　　桐
枇　　　　　　　　　根
树　　　　　　　　　杷
梧　　　　　　　　　花
荷　　　　　　　　　遥

3. 填一填(Blank-filling)

用课文中的汉字填空。

Fill the following blanks with characters in the text.

(1) 每天晚上爷爷都会去公_____散散步。

(2) 一到秋天,树_____都黄了。

(3) 张丽丽见到李华,高兴地向他_____手。

4. 标一标(Marking)

给下面的词组标注拼音。

Mark the following phrases in pinyin.

_____　　　　_____　　　　_____
逍遥　　　　云霄　　　　梧桐

5. 说一说(Talking)

根据所给场景,编写对话并练习。

Based on the given situations, make dialogues and practice.

请说一说你最喜欢的一种植物是什么?为什么?

....

....

....

花中四君子

花中四君子,分别指梅、兰、竹、菊,它们有着与众不同的人格象征。其中,梅迎寒而开,美丽绝俗,而且具有傲霜斗雪的特征,是坚韧不拔的象征。兰,一则花朵色淡香清,二则多生于幽僻之处,故常被看作谦谦君子的象征。竹,也经冬不凋,且自成美景,它刚直、谦逊,不卑不亢,潇洒处世,常被看作不同流俗的高雅之士的象征。菊,清丽淡雅、芳香怡人,不与群芳争艳,故常用于象征恬然自得、傲然不屈的高尚品格。

The Four Gentlemen of Flowers, i. e. plum, orchid, bamboo, and chrysanthemum, symbolize a distinctive personality respectively. The plum, beautiful and bright, blossoming in cold winter and defying frost and snow, symbolizes the spirit of perseverance. With its light color and fragrant scent, growing in quiet and remote places, orchids are often seen as a symbol of modesty. Bamboos, green even in winter and having their own beauty, always standing straight and unassuming, are often seen as a symbol of elegance. The chrysanthemum, elegant and fragrant, in full bloom even after other flowers have withered, has traditionally been used to symbolize the noble character of being calm and unyielding.

第二十课　耽读玩市

Lesson Twenty   Indulging in Reading in the Market

1. 描红并注音(Trace strokes and add pinyin)

2. 话题导入(Topic introduction)

你认为多读书有哪些好处？
What do you think are the benefits of reading more books?

耽　读　玩　市，寓　目　囊　箱。
Dān① dú wán shì② yù mù náng③ xiāng

易　輶　攸　畏，属　耳　垣　墙。
Yì yóu④ yōu wèi⑤ zhǔ ěr yuán⑥ qiáng

具　膳　餐　饭，适　口　充　肠。
Jù⑦ shàn cān fàn shì kǒu chōng cháng

饱　饫　烹　宰，饥　厌　糟　糠。
Bǎo yù⑧ pēng zǎi jī yàn⑨ zāo kāng

亲　戚　故　旧，老　少　异　粮。
Qīn qī gù jiù lǎo shào yì liáng

1. 注释(Notes)

①耽：沉溺(indulge)。

②玩市：热闹的集市(busy market)。

③囊：口袋(pocket)。

④輶：一种轻便的车子(a light carriage)。

⑤攸畏：有所畏惧(fear)。

⑥垣：矮墙，也泛指墙(wall)。

⑦具：准备(prepare)。

⑧饫：厌倦(bored)。

⑨厌：满足(satisfy)，如："学而不厌,诲人不倦,何有于我哉？"。

2. 原文大意(Paraphrase)

汉代王充在街市上沉迷于读书不能自拔,眼睛看到的都是他的书袋和书箱。
换了轻便的车子要注意安全,说话要防止隔墙有耳。
平时的饭菜,要适合口味让人吃得饱。
吃饱时大鱼大肉都不想吃,饿时粗菜淡饭都很满足。
聚会时要盛情款待亲属、朋友,老人、小孩的食物应该与自己的不一样。

三 汉字学习 Chinese character

千字文

箱

拼音	xiāng
词性	名词(n.)
释义	盛东西的工具(box)
搭配	行李箱(suitcase)
例句	我的书都放在行李箱里了。All my books are in the suitcase.

易

拼音	yì
词性	形容词(adj.)
释义	轻易的(easy)
搭配	容易(easy)
例句	写好汉字不是一件容易的事。 It's not easy to write Chinese characters well.

耳

拼音	ěr
词性	名词(n.)
释义	听觉和平衡感觉的器官(organ)
搭配	耳朵(ear)
例句	兔子的耳朵很长。 Rabbit's ears are very long.

具

拼音	jù
词性	动词(v.)
释义	备有(be equipped with)
搭配	具备(possess; have)
例句	你具备我们需要的一切优秀品质。 You have all the good qualities we need.

充

拼音	chōng
词性	动词(v.)
释义	填满,装满(fill);当,担任(be)
搭配	充满(fill)
例句	教室里充满了欢声笑语。 The classroom was full of happy songs and laughter.

厌

拼音	yàn
词性	形容词(adj.)
释义	不喜欢(dislike)
搭配	贪得无厌(greedy);讨厌(hate)
例句	我们不能做贪得无厌的人。 We can't be greedy.

肠

拼音	cháng
词性	名词(n.)
释义	人或动物的内脏(the internal organs of a person or an animal)
搭配	心肠(heart)

例句	她有一副好心肠，对每个人都很热情。 She has a good heart and is very warm to everyone.

亲

拼音	qīn
词性	名词（n.）
释义	有血统或姻亲关系的（related by blood or marriage）
搭配	亲人，亲戚（relative）
例句	他是我的远方亲戚。 He is a distant relative of mine.

旧

拼音	jiù
词性	形容词（adj.）
释义	过去认识的人（people known before）；过去的（old）
搭配	旧书（secondhand book）
例句	旧书市场里有很多好书。 There are many good books in the secondhand book market.

粮

拼音	liáng
词性	名词（n.）
释义	可吃的谷类、豆类等（eatable cereals, beans, etc.）
搭配	粮食（food）
例句	我们离不开粮食。We can't do without food.

(一) 你读过哪本书？(Which book have you read?)

Lǐ Huá：Nǐ dú guo zhōng wén shū jí ma
李 华：你读过中文书籍吗？

Zhāng Lì li：Wǒ dú guo sān zì jīng
张丽丽：我读过《三字经》。

Lǐ Huá：Nǐ jué de zěn me yàng
李 华：你觉得怎么样？

Zhāng Lì li：Wǒ jué de hěn yǒu qù，nǐ yě kě yǐ shì yi shì
张丽丽：我觉得很有趣，你也可以试一试。

Lǐ Huá：Hǎo de xiè xie nǐ
李 华：好的，谢谢你。

Zhāng Lì li：Bú kè qi
张丽丽：不客气。

(二) 你喜欢吃中国菜吗？(Do you like Chinese food?)

Liú Fāng：Nǐ xǐ huan chī zhōng guó cài ma
刘 芳：你喜欢吃中国菜吗？

Chén Shì jié：Wǒ hěn xǐ huan，zuì xǐ huan suān là tǔ dòu sī，nǐ ne
陈士杰：我很喜欢，最喜欢酸辣土豆丝，你呢？

Liú Fāng：Wǒ yě shì，wǒ yě hěn xǐ huan suān là tǔ dòu sī
刘 芳：我也是，我也很喜欢酸辣土豆丝。

Chén Shì jié：Wǒ zhī dao yí gè cān tīng zuò de suān là tǔ dòu sī tè bié hǎo chī
陈士杰：我知道一个餐厅做的酸辣土豆丝特别好吃。

Liú Fāng：Zhēn de ma Wǒ men yì qǐ qù ba
刘 芳：真的吗？我们一起去吧！

Chén Shì jié：Hǎo Wǒ men zǒu ba
陈士杰：好！我们走吧。

1. 副词(从来)

用法：用在动词或形容词前面，表示动作、行为或情况从过去到现在没有变化。

句型：主语＋从来＋动词/形容词(＋宾语)。

例句：我从来没吃过法国菜。

他从来不去游泳。

2. 简单趋向补语

用法：动词"来"和"去"用在一些动词后做补语，表动作趋向。

句型：主语＋动词＋（宾语）＋来/去（了）。

例句：他出去了。

他回美国去了。

老师回家去了。

1. 写一写(Writing)

根据拼音写汉字。

Write down the corresponding characters according to pinyin.

yì　　　　　　　jù　　　　　　　jiù
容____　　　____备　　　____书

2. 连一连(Matching)

把右列的汉字与左列的汉字相连组词。

Match characters in the right column with one in the left column to form a phrase.

箱　　　　　　　易
充　　　　　　　子
容　　　　　　　戚
亲　　　　　　　朵
耳　　　　　　　满

3. 说一说(Talking)

请比较下列词语并进行造句练习。

Compare the following phrases, make dialogues and practice.

（1）……喜欢……

例句：刘芳喜欢吃蔬菜水果，因为蔬菜水果很健康。

（2）……觉得……

例句：刘芳觉得蔬菜水果很健康，所以她喜欢吃。

4. 默一默(Writing from memory)

根据课文内容填空。

Fill in the blanks according to the text.

耽读玩_____，寓_____囊箱。

_____辄攸畏，属_____垣墙。

_____膳餐饭，适_____充肠。

饱饫烹宰，饥_____糟糠。

亲戚_____ _____，_____ _____异粮。

5. 填一填(Blank-filling)

用适当的汉字填空。

Fill the following blanks with proper characters.

（1）_____书市场里有很多好书。

（2）她的心_____非常好，对每个人都很热情。

（3）教室里_____满了欢声笑语。

（4）他是我的远房亲_____。

（5）每个人都离不开_____食。

延伸学习 Extended reading

京 剧

京剧是中国五大戏曲剧种之一，是中国的国粹，是中国和世界的非物质文化遗产。京剧场景布置注重写意，腔(qiāng) 调(diào) 以西皮、二黄为主，用胡琴和锣(luó) 鼓(gǔ) 等伴奏。京剧是清代四大徽(huī)班进入北京 融(róng)合昆曲、秦腔的曲目和方法，吸收地方民间曲调，不断改进以后的结晶。

Peking Opera is one of China's five major operas, the quintessence of China, and the intangible cultural heritage of China and the world. The layout of Peking Opera scenes focuses on freehand brushwork. The music and intonation for Peking Opera are chiefly Xipi and Erhuang, accompanied by Huqin and gongs and drums. It is the crystallization of Anhui Opera, Kunqu, and Qinqiang by blending their dramas and methods together and assimilating the music and intonations from local operas after four major theatrical troupes of Anhui Opera were summoned to Peking(former name of Beijing) to celebrate the birthday of the emperor in the Qing Dynasty.

第二十一课　妾御绩纺

Lesson Twenty-one　Concubines and Servants Should Do the Housework

1. 描红并注音(Trace strokes and add pinyin)

( )
巾

( )
夕

( )
象

( )
床

( )
酒

( )
手

2. 话题导入（Topic introduction）

谈谈在你的国家如何庆祝生日。

How do people celebrate birthdays in your country?

Qiè	yù	jì	fǎng①	shì	jīn	wéi	fáng②
妾	御	绩	纺 ，	侍	巾	帷	房 。

Wán③	shàn	yuán	jié④	yín	zhú	wěi	huáng⑤
纨	扇	圆	絜 ，	银	烛	炜	煌 。

Zhòu	mián	xī	mèi	lán	sǔn⑥	xiàng	chuáng
昼	眠	夕	寐 ，	蓝	笋	象	床 。

Xián	gē	jiǔ	yàn	jiē	bēi	jǔ	shāng⑦
弦	歌	酒	宴 ，	接	杯	举	觞 。

Jiǎo	shǒu	dùn	zú	yuè	yù	qiě	kāng
矫	手	顿	足 ，	悦	豫	且	康 。

1. 注释（Notes）

①绩纺：泛指纺纱、绩麻这些事（spinning）。

②帷房：内房，闺房（boudoir）。

③纨：很细的丝织品（fine silk fabric）。

④絜：洁，干净（clean）。

⑤炜煌：明亮又辉煌（bright and brilliant）。

⑥蓝笋：青色的竹席（cyan bamboo mat）。

⑦觞：酒杯（wine glass）。

2. 原文大意（Paraphrase）

妻妾婢女要纺纱织麻，尽心恭敬地服侍好丈夫。

洁白素雅的圆扇，白白的蜡烛明亮辉煌。

白天休息，晚上睡觉，有青篾编成的竹席和象牙雕屏的床。

奏着乐，唱着歌，参加酒宴；接过酒杯，开怀畅饮。

情不自禁地跳起舞来，真是快乐又安康。

三 汉字学习 Chinese character

巾

拼音	jīn
词性	名词(n.)
释义	擦东西或包东西的用品(towel)
搭配	毛巾(towel)
例句	我买了一条新毛巾。I bought a new towel.

扇

拼音	shàn
词性	名词(n.)
释义	扇子(fan)
搭配	扇子(fan)
例句	他送我一把很漂亮的扇子。 He gave me a beautiful fan.

圆

拼音	yuán
词性	形容词(adj.)
释义	从中心点到周边任何一点都相等的图形(circle)
搭配	团圆(reunion)
例句	春节时,中国人会回到家里和家人一起吃团圆饭。 During the Spring Festival, Chinese people return home to have a reunion dinner with their families.

眠

拼音	mián
词性	动词(v.)
释义	睡觉(sleep)
搭配	失眠(insomnia)
例句	我昨晚失眠了。I did not sleep well last night.

夕 ノ 勹 夕

拼音	xī
词性	名词(n.)
释义	黄昏;傍晚(dusk)
搭配	夕阳(sunset)
例句	我喜欢在海边看夕阳。 I like to watch the sunset by the beach.

象 ノ 勹 勹 夕 冉 备 争 争 象 象 象

拼音	xiàng
词性	名词(n.)
释义	一种哺乳动物(elephant)
搭配	大象(elephant)
例句	大象的牙齿非常珍贵。 Elephants' tusks are very valuable.

宴 ` 丶 宀 宀 宀 宁 审 审 宴 宴 宴

拼音	yàn
词性	名词(n.)
释义	酒席(feast)
搭配	宴会(banquet)
例句	宴会来了很多宾客。 Many guests came to the banquet.

举

拼音	jǔ
词性	动词(v.)
释义	推荐(recommend);使升高(lift)
搭配	选举(recommend sb.);举重(weightlifting)
例句	他被选举为班长。 He was elected monitor of the class.

顿

拼音	dùn
词性	动词(v.)
释义	碰、跺(touch);在很短的时间内停止(pause)
搭配	顿足(stamp);停顿(pause)
例句	他讲话时突然停顿了一下。 He paused suddenly during his speech.

足

拼音	zú
词性	名词(n.);形容词(adj.);动词(v.)
释义	脚(foot);充实(adequate);达到要求(meet the requirement)
搭配	足球(football);充足(ample);满足(satisfy)
例句	他喜欢踢足球。 She likes playing soccer.

豫

拼音	yù

续表

词性	形容词(adj.)
释义	快乐(happy)
搭配	犹豫(hesitate)
例句	他在犹豫要不要去看电影。 He is hesitating over whether to go to cinema.

四 日常对话 Dialogue

(一) 锻炼身体(Exercise)

李　华：你喜欢锻炼身体吗？
Lǐ　Huá Nǐ xǐ huan duàn liàn shēn tǐ ma

张丽丽：是的，我很喜欢。
Zhāng Lì li Shì de wǒ hěn xǐ huan

李　华：你最喜欢什么运动呢？
Lǐ　Huá Nǐ zuì xǐ huan shén me yùn dòng ne

张丽丽：我最喜欢跑步，你呢？
Zhāng Lì li Wǒ zuì xǐ huan pǎo bù nǐ ne

李　华：我最喜欢滑雪。
Lǐ　Huá Wǒ zuì xǐ huan huá xuě

张丽丽：哇！那听起来很酷。下次我可以和你一起去吗？
Zhāng Lì li Wā Nà tīng qǐ lai hěn kù Xià cì wǒ kě yǐ hé nǐ yì qǐ qù ma

李　华：好啊。
Lǐ　Huá Hǎo a

(二) 春游(Sight-seeing in spring)

刘　芳：你周末有空吗？我们一起去春游吧！
Liú　Fāng Nǐ zhōu mò yǒu kòng ma Wǒ men yì qǐ qù chūn yóu ba

陈士杰：好啊！你打算去哪里？
Chén Shì jié Hǎo a Nǐ dǎ suàn qù nǎ lǐ

刘　芳：去校园湖边怎么样？
Liú　Fāng Qù xiào yuán hú biān zěn me yàng

陈士杰：我听说樱花都开了。
Chén Shì jié Wǒ tīng shuō yīng huā dōu kāi le

刘　芳：是的，非常漂亮，我们一起去享受春光吧！
Liú　Fāng Shì de fēi cháng piào liang wǒ men yì qǐ qù xiǎng shòu chūn guāng ba

1. 比较句 1

用法：比较句—带程度补语/情态补语。

句型：A＋比 B＋形容词/动词 ＋程度/情态补语。

例句：最近香蕉比苹果便宜得多。

他比我写得好。

他写汉字比我写得好多了。

2. 比较句 2

用法：表示程度的累进，"一"的后面也可以替换为其他量词，例如，一天比一天、一次比一次、一年比一年等。

句型：一天比一天。

例句：天气一天比一天热了。

女儿的数学考试一次比一次好。

这儿的环境一年比一年好了。

1. 写一写(Writing)

根据拼音写汉字。

Write down the corresponding characters according to pinyin.

jīn	xiàng	jiǔ
毛＿＿＿	＿＿＿牙	＿＿＿杯

2. 连一连(Matching)

把右列的汉字与左列的汉字相连组词。

Match characters in the right column with one in the left column to form a phrase.

安	子
停	康
失	顿
团	眠
扇	圆

3. 填一填(Blank-filling)

用适当的汉字填空。

Fill the following blanks with proper characters.

(1) 他在犹_____要不要去看电影。

(2) 他参加了班长的选_____,最后他成功了。

(3) _____会来了很多宾客。

(4) 他非常喜欢踢_____球。

用下面给出的词语填空。

Fill the following blanks with characters given below.

　　　　而且　　夕阳　　敢　　关于　　毛巾　　众多

(1) 妈妈买了一条新的(　　　)。

(2) 他(　　　)于挑战学习中的困难。

(3) 李红不仅歌唱得好,(　　　)字写得也漂亮。

(4) 美丽的城市吸引了(　　　)游客。

(5) (　　　)这个话题,今天就谈到这里。

(6) 快看,现在的(　　　)真美。

4. 默一默(Writing from memory)

根据课文内容填空。

Fill in the blanks according to the text.

妾御绩纺,侍_____帷房。

纨扇_____絜,_____烛炜煌。

昼眠夕寐,_____笋_____床。

弦歌_____宴,_____杯举觞。

矫_____顿_____,悦豫且_____。

5. 说一说(Talking)

根据所给场景,编写对话并练习。

Based on the given situations, make dialogues and practice.

说一说最近天气的变化,你有什么出行的打算吗?

Talk about the recent changes in the weather. Do you have any plans to travel?

提示:比较句(一天比一天)

黄 河

黄河是中国第二长河,中华文明最主要的发源地,被称作中国人的"母亲河"。青藏高原巴颜喀拉山脉是黄河的发源地,黄河呈"几"字形,最终流入渤海,黄河干流全长约5464公里,流域面积约75.2万平方公里。由于中段流经黄土高原地区夹带了大量泥沙,所以它也是世界上含沙量最多的河流。

The Yellow River, the second longest river in China and the main birthplace of Chinese civilization, is called "the mother river" of Chinese people. The Bayan Har Mountains of the Qinghai-Tibet Plateau is the birthplace of the Yellow River. The mainstream of the Yellow River, in the shape of an inverted "U" and with a length of about 5,464 kilometers, eventually flows into the Bohai Sea, covering a watershed area of about 752,000 square kilometers. Due to the fact that its middle section flows through the Loess Plateau, taking a lot of loess along, it is also the river with the highest sand content in the world.

第二十二课　嫡后嗣续

Lesson Twenty-two　Descendants and Inheritance

1. 描红并注音(Trace strokes and add pinyin)

( )
后

( )
尝

( )
拜

( )
简

简

( )
要

( )

2. 话题导入（Topic introduction）

你了解过中国古代有哪些礼仪吗？
Have you ever learned any etiquette in ancient China?

嫡① 后 嗣 续，祭 祀 烝 尝②。
稽颡③ 再 拜，悚 惧 恐 惶。
笺④ 牒 简 要，顾 答 审 详。
骸⑤ 垢 想 浴，执 热 愿 凉。
驴 骡 犊 特，骇 跃 超 骧⑥。

1. 注释（Notes）

①嫡：奴隶社会、封建社会中的正妻（official wife in feudal society）。
②烝尝：代指一年四季的祭祀（sacrifice of the four seasons）。
③稽颡：屈膝下拜，以额触地（kowtow）。
④笺：文书、书信（letter）。
⑤骸：身体（body）。
⑥骧：马抬起头快跑（gallop）。

2. 原文大意（Paraphrase）

子孙继承了祖先的基业，一年四季的祭祀大礼不能忘记。
跪着磕头，拜了又拜；礼仪要周全恭敬，心情要悲痛虔诚。
给别人写信要简明扼要，回答别人问题要详细周全。
身上有了污垢，就想洗澡，好比手上拿着烫的东西就希望有风把它吹凉。
家里有了灾祸，连牲畜都会受惊，狂蹦乱跳，东奔西跑。

三 汉字学习 Chinese character

续

拼音	xù
词性	动词(v.)
释义	接连不断(incessant)
搭配	持续(last)
例句	这个活动还要持续几个月。 This activity will last for several months.

尝

拼音	cháng
词性	动词(v.)
释义	辨别食物的味道(identify the taste of food)
搭配	品尝(taste)
例句	请你来品尝一下这个菜。Please taste this dish.

恐

拼音	kǒng
词性	动词(v.)
释义	害怕;畏惧(fear)
搭配	恐惧(fear)
例句	听到尖叫声,我非常恐惧。 I was very frightened when I heard the scream.

拜

拼音	bài

词性	动词(v.)
释义	行礼表示敬意(salute)
搭配	拜访(visit)
例句	我打算周末去拜访赵老师。 I'm going to visit Miss Zhao at the weekend.

拼音	jiǎn
词性	形容词(adj.)
释义	明白清晰的(clear)
搭配	简单(simple)
例句	我喜欢简单的装修风格。 I prefer a simple style of decoration.

拼音	xiáng
词性	形容词(adj.)
释义	细致的(detailed)
搭配	详细(detailed);详尽(full and exhaustive)
例句	这份清单非常详细。 This list is full and exhaustive.

拼音	zhí
词性	动词(v.)
释义	拿着(hold)

搭配	执行（carry out）
例句	制定的法律必须严格执行。 Laws enacted must be strictly enforced.

四 日常对话 Dialogue

（一）过生日（Birthday celebration）

李　华：丽丽，祝你生日快乐！

张丽丽：谢谢，欢迎你来参加我的生日聚会。

李　华：你过生日许愿了吗？

张丽丽：我还没有把生日蛋糕拿出来。

李　华：你许愿的时候我给你拍照。

张丽丽：谢谢。

（二）逛超市（Visiting a supermarket）

陈士杰：刘芳，今天有时间一起去逛超市吧？

刘　芳：好啊，我来中国还没有去过超市。

陈士杰：这是我这个月去的第三趟。

刘　芳：我们可以去买点儿菜。

陈士杰：下午五点在学校门口见。

刘　芳：好的，到时候见。

五 语法知识 Grammar

1. 把字句

用法：汉语句式的一种，用介词"把"构成的介宾短语做状语的句子。

句型:(主语+)把+宾语+动作。

例句:请把空调打开。

　　　把电脑关了。

　　　他把地图贴在了墙上。

2. 动量词(遍、趟、次、回、顿等)

用法:表示动作行为的单位。

例句:这本书我看了三遍。

　　　我去了三趟超市。

　　　因为我迟到了,老师把我批评了一顿。

1. 写一写(Writing)

根据拼音写汉字。

Write down the corresponding characters according to pinyin.

　　cháng　　　　　dān　　　　　fǎng
品_____　　　简_____　　　拜_____

2. 连一连(Matching)

把右列的汉字与左列的汉字相连组词。

Match characters in the right column with one in the left column to form a phrase.

详　　　　　　　　　　　惧

持　　　　　　　　　　　细

恐　　　　　　　　　　　续

执　　　　　　　　　　　单

简　　　　　　　　　　　行

3. 填一填(Blank-filling)

用适当的汉字填空。

Fill the following blanks with proper characters.

(1) 你过生日许_____了吗?

(2) 我还没有_____生日蛋糕拿出来。

(3) 这是我这个月去的第三_____。

4. 默一默(Writing from memory)

根据课文内容填空。

Fill in the blanks according to the text.

嫡_____嗣_____，祭_____祀_____。

稽颡_____ _____，悚_____恐_____。

_____牒_____要，顾答_____ _____。

5. 说一说(Talking)

根据所给场景，编写对话并练习。

Based on the given situations, make dialogues and practice.

运用下列词语造句，并和同伴进行对话练习。

提示：过生日、拜访、超市、详细、品尝

七 延伸学习 Extended reading

中国传统家庭教育

中国传统家庭教育，往往把孩子的行为习惯和品德(pǐn dé)教育(jiào yù)放在第一位，将培养孩子成为一个有良知、能自立、懂孝(xiào)道、有责任心的人作为家庭教育的首要任务。中国传统观念认为良好的品德是与人交往、取得成功的关键(jiàn)。很多家庭在孩子小的时候就告知其在外面要待人恭(gōng)敬(jìng)，讲求诚信；在家里要尊(zūn)敬长辈(bèi)、爱护幼小，平时要秉(bǐng)持(chí)勤(qín)奋(fèn)俭(jiǎn)朴(pǔ)、不求奢(shē)侈(chǐ)的生活方式。这些优秀的教育传统长期以来为历代家庭继承和借鉴(jiàn)，在当代中国家庭教育和人才培养方面仍发挥着重要作用。

In traditional Chinese family education, children's behavior and moral education are often placed in the first place. The primary task of family education is to cultivate their child to be a person with conscience, self-reliance, filial piety and sense of responsibility. Traditional Chinese families believe that having a good character is the key to communicating with others and achieving success. Many families teach their children from an early age to be respectful and honest outside. and to revere the elders and care for the young at home, try to always maintain diligent and frugal and do not pursue luxury lifestyles. These excellent educational traditions have long been inherited and used for reference by many families, and still play an important role in family education and personnel training in contemporary China.

第二十三课　诛斩贼盗

Lesson Twenty-three　Eradication of Thieves and Bandits

1. 描红并注音(Trace strokes and add pinyin)

( )
亡

( )
笔

( )
利

( )
毛

( )
工

( )
笑

2. 话题导入(Topic introduction)

你知道中国有哪些发明家吗？他们都发明了些什么？
Do you know any inventors in China? What have they invented?

诛斩贼盗，捕获叛亡。
Zhū zhǎn zéi dào, bǔ huò pàn wáng.

布①射 僚②丸，嵇③琴 阮④啸。
Bù shè Liáo wán, Jī qín Ruǎn xiào.

恬⑤笔 伦⑥纸，钧⑦巧 任⑧钓。
Tián bǐ Lún zhǐ, Jūn qiǎo Rén diào.

释纷利俗，并皆佳妙。
Shì fēn lì sú, bìng jiē jiā miào.

毛⑨施⑩淑姿，工⑪颦⑫妍笑。
Máo Shī shū zī, gōng pín yán xiào.

1. 注释(Notes)

①布：吕布，擅长射箭(Lü Bu, good at archery)。

②僚：熊宜僚，善玩弹丸(Xiong Yiliao, good at playing with pellets)。

③嵇：嵇康，"竹林七贤"之一(Ji Kang, one of "the Seven Sages of the Bamboo Grove")。

④阮：阮籍，"竹林七贤"之一(Ruan Ji, one of "the Seven Sages of the Bamboo Grove")。

⑤恬：蒙恬，改良毛笔(Meng Tian, improved the writing brush)。

⑥伦：蔡伦，改进造纸术(Cai Lun, improved papermaking technology)。

⑦钧：马钧，龙骨水车等的发明家(Ma Jun, inventor of the dragon bone watermill, etc.)。

⑧任：任父，传说中善钓的神人(Ren Fu, a legendary god proficient at fishing)。

⑨毛：毛嫱，中国古代美女(Mao Qiang, a beauty in ancient China)。

⑩施：西施，中国古代美女(Xi Shi, a beauty in ancient China)。

⑪工：善于(skillful, proficient)。

⑫颦：皱眉(frown)。

2. 原文大意(Paraphrase)

官府杀死盗贼，追捕叛逆逃亡的坏人，这样才能消除隐患。

吕布擅长射箭,宜僚善于玩弹丸,嵇康善于弹琴,阮籍善于撮口长啸。

蒙恬改良毛笔,蔡伦改进造纸术,马钧巧制水车,任公子善于钓鱼。

他们的技艺有的解人纠纷,有的方便群众,都高明巧妙,为人称道。

毛嫱、西施年轻美貌,哪怕皱着眉头,也像美美的笑。

拼音	huò
词性	动词(v.)
释义	得到(obtain)
搭配	获得(get)
例句	他的努力获得了回报。His efforts paid off in the end.

拼音	bù
词性	动词(v.)
释义	宣告,对众陈述(declare)
搭配	宣布(declare)
例句	该公司已经宣布破产。The company has declared bankruptcy.

拼音	shè
词性	动词(v.)
释义	用推力或弹力送出子弹等(use thrust or elastic force to send out bullets, etc.)
搭配	发射(launch)

| 例句 | 为了确保卫星发射成功,科学家们日夜辛勤工作。
In order to ensure the success of the satellite launch, scientists worked hard day and night. |

琴

拼音	qín
词性	名词(n.)
释义	一类乐器的统称(collective title for a group of musical instruments)
搭配	钢琴(piano)
例句	张老师正在教学生弹钢琴。 Miss Zhang is teaching her students to play the piano.

巧

拼音	qiǎo
词性	形容词(adj.)
释义	技艺高明(high skill)
搭配	巧妙(ingenious)
例句	他设计了一个巧妙的实验。 He has designed an ingenious experiment.

任

拼音	rén;rèn
词性	姓(n.);动词(v.)
释义	负担,担当(take on)
搭配	担任(undertake)
例句	他担任了这个职务。He undertook the post.

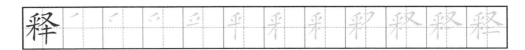

拼音	shì
词性	动词(v.)
释义	放开(let go)
搭配	释放(release)
例句	他最终被无罪释放。He was finally acquitted.

拼音	fēn
词性	形容词(adj.)
释义	众多,杂乱(numerous and messy)
搭配	纷纷(one after another)
例句	由于严重的经济危机,企业、银行纷纷倒闭。Due to the serious economic crisis, enterprises and banks have closed down one after another.

拼音	sú
词性	名词(n.)
释义	社会上长期形成的风尚、礼节、习惯等(custom)
搭配	风俗、习俗(custom)
例句	罗马人保护文物,几乎成为一种风俗。It was almost a custom for the Romans to protect cultural relics.

四 日常对话 Dialogue

（一）兴趣爱好（Hobbies）

张丽丽：李华，你平时都有哪些兴趣爱好？

李　华：我喜欢各项体育活动，尤其是射击。

张丽丽：射击肯定很有趣。

李　华：是的。你喜欢做什么？

张丽丽：我热爱音乐，最喜欢弹钢琴。

李　华：你平时参加钢琴比赛吗？

张丽丽：当然。这个周末我就有一场比赛。

李　华：那太好了！到时候我一定去看。

（二）音乐会（Concert）

刘　芳：这周六我打算去听音乐会，你想和我一起去吗？

陈士杰：真的吗？我早就想去听音乐会了，我以前没听过。

刘　芳：音乐会在阳光剧院，周六下午两点开始。

陈士杰：哇，那太好了！到时候我和你一起去。

刘　芳：好。我已经迫不及待了。

陈士杰：那我们周六下午一点半在剧院门口见。

刘　芳：好的。我现在就去买票。

五 语法知识 Grammar

1. 选择复句（未定选择）

用法：复句的几个分句提出几种情况或一件事情的几个方面，让人从中选择，但说话者并未有所取舍。

未定选择常用的关联词语是：

单用：或者、或是、或、还是。

合用：或者（或、或是）……，或者（或、或是）……；是……，还是……；要么……，要么……"。

句型：或者……，或者……。

例句：你要么别去说，要么就说个明白。

是同学们自立的意识强了，还是其他什么原因？

要么被困难吓倒，要么漠视困难的存在，要么就拿出勇气来战胜困难。

2. 程度副词（更）

用法：程度副词是对动词、形容词或副词在程度上加以限定或修饰的副词。一般位置在被修饰的形容词或者副词之前。

句型：更＋动词/形容词/副词。

例句：我现在比以前更喜欢看书了。

现在他打篮球打得更好了。

比起以前，现在城市的环境更好了。

六 课后练习 Exercises

1. 写一写（Writing）

根据拼音写汉字。

Write down the corresponding characters according to pinyin.

  huò   bù   qiǎo   rèn

____得 宣____ ____妙 担____

2. 连一连(Matching)

把右列的汉字与左列的汉字相连组词。

Match characters in the right column with one in the left column to form a phrase.

巧	放
发	任
释	妙
担	射
纷	俗
庸	纷

3. 填一填(Blank-filling)

用适当的汉字填空。

Fill the following blanks with proper characters.

（1）小芳在这节物理课上_____得了很多知识。
（2）班主任走进教室,宣_____了此次比赛的结果。
（3）经过长时间的练习,她终于学会了弹钢_____。
（4）他的组织能力强,在大学期间担_____了很多活动的组织者。
（5）这种物质燃烧后将会_____放出大量有害气体。

4. 默一默(Writing from memory)

根据课文内容填空。

Fill in the blanks according to the text.

诛斩贼盗,捕_____叛亡。

_____ _____僚丸,嵇_____阮啸。

恬笔伦纸,钧_____ _____钓。

_____纷利_____,并皆佳妙。

5. 说一说(Talking)

根据所给场景,编写对话并练习。

Based on the given situations, make dialogues and practice.

询问自己同学或朋友的课余爱好。

提示:或者……,或者……;更

七 延伸学习 Extended reading

四大名绣

四大名绣,指的是我国刺绣中的苏州苏绣、湖南湘绣、广东粤绣和四川蜀绣。刺绣就是用针将丝线或其他纤维、纱线以一定图案和色彩在绣料上穿刺,以绣迹构成花纹的装饰织物。它是用针和线把人的设计和制作添加在任何存在的织物上的一种艺术。中国的刺绣工艺在秦汉(前221—220)时期便已达到较高水平,是历史上"丝绸之路"中运输的重要商品之一。四大名绣是中国刺绣的突出代表。

The four famous embroideries refer to Suzhou, Hunan, Guangdong and Sichuan embroideries. Embroidery is a kind of decorative fabrics that uses needles to puncture silk threads or other fibers and yarns on the embroidered material with certain patterns and colors to form patterns. It is an art of adding human design and production to any existing fabric with needles and threads. China's embroidery technology reached a high level in the Qin and Han Dynasties(221 B.C.-220 A.D.), and it was one of the important commodities transported along the "Silk Road" in history. China's four famous embroideries are outstanding representatives of Chinese embroidery.

第二十四课　年矢每催

Lesson Twenty-four　Time Pressing Forward

1. 描红并注音(Trace strokes and add pinyin)

( )
年

( )
矢

( )
每

( )
步

( )
闻

( )
语

2. 话题导入(Topic introduction)

谈谈你在《千字文》学习过程中的收获。

Talk about what you have learned from ***Qian Zi Wen***(*One-Thousand-Character Essay*).

Nián	shǐ①	měi	cuī	xī	huī	lǎng	yào②
年	矢	每	催，	曦	晖	朗	曜。
Xuán	jī③	xuán	wò④	huì	pò⑤	huán	zhào
璇	玑	悬	斡，	晦	魄	环	照。
Zhǐ	xīn⑥	xiū	hù⑦	yǒng	suí⑧	jí	shào⑨
指	薪	修	祜，	永	绥	吉	劭。
Jǔ	bù	yǐn	lǐng	fǔ	yǎng	láng	miào
矩	步	引	领，	俯	仰	廊	庙。
Shù	dài	jīn⑩	zhuāng	pái	huái	zhān	tiào
束	带	矜	庄，	徘	徊	瞻	眺。
Gū	lòu	guǎ	wén	yú	méng	děng	qiào
孤	陋	寡	闻，	愚	蒙	等	诮。
Wèi	yǔ	zhù	zhě	yān	zāi	hū	yě
谓	语	助	者，	焉	哉	乎	也。

1. 注释(Notes)

①矢：箭(arrow)。

②曜：日光(sunlight)；照耀(shine)。

③璇玑：古代称北斗星的第一星至第四星(the first four stars of the Plough)。

④斡：旋转(spin)。

⑤晦魄：月亮(moon)。

⑥指薪：把动物脂肪用作燃料，此处引申为"薪火相传"(fat used as firewood; here it refers to the inheritance passing from generation to generation)。

⑦祜：福(bliss)。

⑧绥：安定(stable)；和平(peace)。

⑨劭：美好的品质(good quality)。

⑩矜：自夸(boast)。

2. 原文大意(Paraphrase)

青春易逝，岁月催人老，只有太阳的光辉永远朗照。

216

高悬的北斗星随着四季变换转动,明晦的月光洒遍人间每个角落。
行善积德才能像薪尽火传那样精神长存,子孙安康全靠你留下吉祥的忠告。
如此心地坦然,方可以昂头迈步,应付朝廷委以的重任。
衣带穿着整齐端庄,举止从容,高瞻远瞩。
这些道理孤陋寡闻就不会明白,只能和愚昧无知的人一样空活一世,让人耻笑。
说到古书中的语助词,那就是"焉""哉""乎""也"了。

三 汉字学习 Chinese character

朗

拼音	lǎng
词性	形容词(adj.)
释义	明亮(bright)
搭配	明朗(bright, clear)
例句	情况逐渐明朗起来。The situation gradually became clear.

指

拼音	zhǐ
词性	动词(v.)
释义	点名(call the roll);告知(tell)
搭配	指挥(conduct, conductor)
例句	一个乐队只需要一个乐队指挥。 A band only needs a conductor.

修

拼音	xiū
词性	动词(v.)
释义	积累(accumulate)
搭配	修改(modify, modification)

例句	小明的文章需要多次修改。 Xiaoming's article needs much modification.

步

拼音	bù
词性	动词(v.)
释义	走(walk)
搭配	散步(go for a walk)
例句	小明最喜欢晚上跟爸妈去散步。 Xiaoming likes to go for a walk with his parents in the evening.

引

拼音	yǐn
词性	动词(v.)
释义	招来(attract);导致(lead to)
搭配	吸引(attract)
例句	小李被美丽的山水景色吸引了。 Xiaoli was attracted by the beautiful landscape.

领

拼音	lǐng
词性	动词(v.)
释义	引导(guide)
搭配	领导(leader)
例句	他很尊重他的领导。 He shows great respect for his leader.

束

拼音	shù

词性	动词(v.)
释义	捆绑(binding)
搭配	束手无策(at a loss what to do)
例句	面对再先进的设备,没有文化知识的人也只能束手无策。 For the advanced equipment, ignorant people are at a loss what to do with it.

谓

拼音	wèi
词性	动词(v.)
释义	说(say)
搭配	所谓(what is called, so-called)
例句	学会满足,所谓知足者常乐也。 Learn to be content, because a so-called content person is always happy.

乎

拼音	hū
词性	语气词(modal particle)
释义	表示疑问或反问,跟"吗"相同(used to express a question or a rhetorical question)
搭配	几乎(almost)
例句	小明摔倒时几乎要大叫出来。 Xiaoming almost cried out when he fell.

(一)赶时间(Tight time)

张丽丽:从学校到机场很远吗?
Zhāng Lì li: Cóng xué xiào dào jī chǎng hěn yuǎn ma

刘　芳:坐地铁需要一个小时左右,打车半个小时。
Liú Fāng: Zuò dì tiě xū yào yí gè xiǎo shí zuǒ yòu, dǎ chē bàn gè xiǎo shí.

张丽丽：那我不得不打车过去了，我很赶时间。

刘　芳：你的航班是几点的？

张丽丽：晚上七点，现在已经五点半了。

刘　芳：那你快去吧，注意安全。

（二）学汉语（Learning Chinese）

李　华：说说你学汉语有什么收获吧！

陈士杰：对我来说，学汉语让我了解了不同语言之间的差异。

李　华：是的，汉语本身非常有魅力。

陈士杰：对你来说，学汉语有什么收获吗？

李　华：对我来说，学汉语不仅让我会说汉语，还让我更加了解中华文化。

1. 不得不

用法：双重否定带有强调成分，加重语气。

例句：我不得不再买一张票。

　　　因为明天下雨，比赛不得不改时间。

2. 固定句式：对……来说

用法：对……来说，表示站在某一角度看问题。

例句：对每个人来说，生命只有一次。

　　　对中国人来说，春节是最重要的节日。

　　　对我来说，这本书比其他书都要重要。

1. 写一写(Writing)

根据拼音写汉字。

Write down the corresponding characters according to pinyin.

  lǎng   wèi   lǐng
明_____   所_____   _____导

2. 连一连(Matching)

把右列的汉字与左列的汉字相连组词。

Match characters in the right column with one in the left column to form a phrase.

耳   戴
指   缚
吸   甲
佩   引
束   环

3. 填一填(Blank-filling)

用适当的汉字填空。

Fill the following blanks with proper characters.

（1）小明是学校乐队的_____挥。
（2）假期结_____后，小丽去写作业了。
（3）小李很听_____导的话。

4. 默一默(Writing from memory)

根据课文内容填空。

Fill in the blanks according to the text.

矩_____引_____，俯仰_____ _____。
_____ _____矜庄，徘徊瞻眺。
_____陋寡_____，愚蒙等诮。
谓语助_____，焉哉_____也。

5. 说一说(Talking)

根据所给场景，编写对话并练习。
Based on the given situations, make dialogues and practice.
用"对……来说"来讲述自己学习汉语的意义。

_____
_____

中国国画

国画一词起源于汉代，主要指的是画在绢、宣纸(xuān zhǐ)、帛上并加以装裱(zhuāng biǎo)的卷轴画(juàn zhóu)。国画是中国的传统绘画(chuán tǒng huì huà)形式，是用毛笔蘸(zhàn)水、墨、彩作画于绢或纸上。中国画在内容和艺术创作(chuàng zuò)上，体现了古人对自然、社会及与之相关(guān lián)的政治(zhèng zhì)、哲学(zhé xué)、宗教(zōng jiào)、道德(dào dé)、文艺等方面的认知(rèn zhī)。

Chinese painting, originated in the Han Dynasty, mainly refers to the mounted scroll painting painted on silk, rice paper and silk. Chinese painting is a traditional form of painting in China. It is painted on silk or paper with a brush dipped in water, ink or color. In terms of content and artistic creation, Chinese painting embodies the ancients' cognition of nature, society, politics, philosophy, religion, morality, literature, art and so on.

附录一　生字表

宇	1	龙	3	诗	5
洪	1	官	3	悲	5
辰	1	始	3	赞	5
宿	1	制	3	染	5
列	1	民	3	景	6
张	1	汤	3	维	6
寒	1	朝	4	念	6
暑	1	章	4	德	6
藏	1	首	4	建	6
余	1	率	4	立	6
律	1	宾	4	形	6
调	1	归	4	恶	6
致	1	化	4	积	6
露	1	被	4	福	6
金	2	木	4	善	6
丽	2	及	4	庆	6
玉	2	盖	5	尺	6
巨	2	此	5	宝	6
珠	2	敢	5	寸	6
称	2	伤	5	竞	6
光	2	效	5	资	7
珍	2	良	5	父	7
李	2	谈	5	严	7
咸	2	彼	5	敬	7
淡	2	器	5	与	7
羽	2	羊	5	当	7

注：第一列为生字，第二列为课别，共277个生字。

尽	7	叔	9	内	12
命	7	犹	9	达	12
临	7	怀	9	承	12
深	7	连	9	既	12
薄	7	兄	9	集	12
似	7	切	9	聚	12
松	7	投	9	群	12
容	8	规	9	壁	12
止	8	义	10	府	13
辞	8	性	10	将	13
初	8	退	10	户	13
诚	8	性	10	县	13
美	8	神	10	兵	13
终	8	志	10	陪	13
令	8	守	10	振	13
荣	8	逐	10	世	13
基	8	移	10	架	13
籍	8	坚	10	肥	13
甚	8	操	10	策	13
无	8	华	11	功	13
登	8	据	11	阿	14
摄	8	盘	11	曲	14
职	8	惊	11	微	14
政	8	彩	11	旦	14
存	8	舍	11	营	14
益	8	启	11	济	14
尊	9	甲	11	弱	14
夫	9	设	12	扶	14
妇	9	席	12	惠	14
训	9	鼓	12	武	14
傅	9	升	12	密	14
母	9	阶	12	士	14
奉	9	转	12	宁	14
姑	9	疑	12	困	15

224

途	15	居	18	夕	21
土	15	沉	18	象	21
何	15	默	18	宴	21
遵	15	古	19	举	21
约	15	寻	19	顿	21
烦	15	散	19	足	21
军	15	虑	19	豫	21
精	15	欣	19	续	22
宣	15	招	19	尝	22
沙	15	历	19	恐	22
漠	15	抽	19	拜	22
并	16	根	19	简	22
城	16	委	19	详	22
石	16	落	19	执	22
紫	16	叶	19	获	23
池	16	摇	19	布	23
洞	16	独	19	射	23
农	17	摩	20	琴	23
治	17	箱	20	巧	23
艺	17	易	20	任	23
载	17	耳	20	释	23
赏	17	具	20	纷	23
劝	17	充	20	俗	23
史	17	厌	20	朗	24
劳	17	肠	20	指	24
察	18	亲	20	修	24
貌	18	旧	20	步	24
植	18	粮	20	引	24
增	18	巾	21	领	24
极	18	扇	21	束	24
幸	18	圆	21	谓	24
即	18	眠	21	乎	24
林	18				

附录一

附录二 练习参考答案

第一课
1. 律 暑 致 调
2. 陈—列 阳—光 严—寒 收—藏 流—露 多—余
3. (1) 露 (2) 张 (3) 调 (4) 集
4. 日月盈昃,辰宿列张。寒来暑往,秋收冬藏。
5. 略

第二课
1. 金 光 果 淡 羽
2. (1) 丽 (2) 称 (3) 光
3. 金—属 碧—玉 珠—宝 清—淡
4. (1) 金生丽水,玉出昆冈。 (2) 海咸河淡,鳞潜羽翔。
5. 略

第三课
1. 制 民 汤
2. 但—是 龙—头 始—终 人—群 官—方
3. (1) 始 (2) 民 (3) 汤 (4) 官
4. 龙师火帝,鸟官人皇。 始制文字,乃服衣裳。 吊民伐罪,周发殷汤。
5. 略

第四课
1. 率 被 化
2. 平—píng 迩—ěr 草—cǎo 章—zhāng 化—huà

3. (1) 宾 (2) 归 (3) 及 (4) 章
4. 坐朝问道,垂拱平章。 鸣凤在竹,白驹食场。 化被草木,赖及万方。
5. 略

第五课
1. 染 效 赞 悲 诗
2. 勇—敢 彼—此 伤—心 感—染 机—器 谈—判
3. (1) 知道错了一定要改正 (2) 坚持发挥自己的长处 (3) 不议论别人的短处 (4) 不倚仗自己的长处
4. 哭 走 慢慢 看 快快
5. 略

第六课
1. 景 形 维 念 积
2. 品—德 建—设 成—立 善—良 恶—劣 庆—祝 宝—贝
3. (1) 景 (2) 念 (3) 恶 (4) 善
4. (1) 祸因恶积 (2) 福缘善庆 (3) 尺璧非宝 (4) 寸阴是竞
5. 略

第七课
1. 资 命 父
2. 严—格 深—奥 放—松 获—取 资—金
3. (1) 严 (2) 资 (3) 尽 (4) 松
4. 资父事君,曰严与敬。 孝当竭力,忠则尽命。 临深履薄,夙兴温凊。 似兰斯馨,如松之盛。 川流不息,渊澄取映。

5. 略

第八课

1. 安定 诚言
2. 甚—至 无—聊 保—存 优—美 内—存 职—业
3. (1)辞 (2)美 (3)摄 (4)终 (5)甚
4. 容止若思,言辞安定。 笃初诚美,慎终宜令。 荣业所基,籍甚无竟。 学优登仕,摄职从政。 存以甘棠,去而益咏。
5. 略

第九课

1. 妇 怀 兄
2. 母—亲 师—傅 兄—弟 规—定 尊—重
3. (1)叔叔 (2)老师 (3)尊重 (4)还是
4. 乐殊贵贱,礼别尊卑。上和下睦,夫唱妇随。 外受傅训,入奉母仪。诸姑伯叔,犹子比儿。 孔怀兄弟,同气连枝。交友投分,切磨箴规。
5. 略

第十课

1. 持 物 满
2. 满—足 安—静 坚—持 文—物 物—品 心—情
3. (1)坚持 (2)满意 (3)冷静 (4)物品
4. 性静情逸,心动神疲。 守真志满,逐物意移。
5. 略

第十一课

1. 据 彩 华 盘
2. 甲—等 宿—舍 启—发 吃—惊
3. 根据 吃惊 精彩 盘旋
4. 都邑华夏,东西二京。 宫殿盘郁,楼观飞惊。 图写禽兽,画彩仙灵。
5. 略

第十二课

1. 转 集 承 达
2. 既—然 聚—会 承—受 鼓—励 疑—问 设—计
3. (1)路 (2)达 (3)内 (4)转 (5)集 (6)疑
4. 肆筵设席,鼓瑟吹笙。 升阶纳陛,弁转疑星。 右通广内,左达承明。 既集坟典,亦聚群英。 杜稿钟隶,漆书壁经。
5. 略

第十三课

1. 功 陪 富
2. 陪—同 雕—刻 驾—车 富—有 肥—胖
3. (1)住户 (2)陪同 (3)雕刻 (4)功德 (5)肥胖
4. 户封八县,家给千兵。 高冠陪辇,驱毂振缨。 世禄侈富,车驾肥轻。 策功茂实,勒碑刻铭。
5. 略

第十四课

1. 阿 曲 微 旦 营 济 弱
2. 搀—扶 优—惠 武—器 密—切

附录二

227

女—士 宁—可

3. (1)微 (2)营 (3)扶 (4)密

4. 奄宅曲阜,微旦孰营。 桓公匡合,济弱扶倾。

5. 略

第十五课

1. 沙 军 精 宣

2. 任—何 困—难 遵—守 沙—漠 麻—烦 节—约

3. (1)约 (2)土 (3)精 (4)军 (5)遵 (6)困

4. qián tú tǔ dì má fan

5. 略

第十六课

1. 洞 紫 城 并

2. 池—塘 紫—色 石—头 洞—穴 遥—远 城—市

3. (1)城 (2)石 (3)池 (4)紫 (5)洞 (6)并

4. 九州禹迹,百郡秦并。 岳宗泰岱,禅主云亭。 雁门紫塞,鸡田赤城。 昆池碣石,巨野洞庭。 旷远绵邈,岩岫杳冥。

5. 略

第十七课

1. 艺 史 载 劳 治 农

2. 劳—动 农—业 欣—赏 劝—说 历—史

3. (1)劳 (2)载 (3)农

4. quàn shuō zhí shù chén mò

5. 略

第十八课

1. 植 增 幸 沉

千字文

2. (1)居 (2)林 (3)貌

3. 聆音察理,鉴貌辨色。 贻厥嘉猷,勉其祗植。 省躬讥诫,宠增抗极。 殆辱近耻,林皋幸即。 两疏见机,解组谁逼。 索居闲处,沉默寂寥。

4. 邻—居 增—长 沉—默 植—树 森—林

5. 略

第十九课

1. 园 论 叶

2. 逍—遥 枇—杷 树—根 梧—桐 荷—花

3. (1)园 (2)叶 (3)招

4. xiāo yáo yún xiāo wú tóng

5. 略

第二十课

1. 易 具 旧

2. 箱—子 充—满 容—易 亲—戚 耳—朵

3. 略

4. 耽读玩市,寓目囊箱。 易輶攸畏,属耳垣墙。 具膳餐饭,适口充肠。 饱饫烹宰,饥厌糟糠。 亲戚故旧,老少异粮。

5. 旧 肠 充 戚 粮

第二十一课

1. 巾 象 酒

2. 安—康 停—顿 失—眠 团—圆 扇—子

3. (1)豫 (2)举 (3)宴 (4)足
(1)毛巾 (2)敢 (3)而且 (4)众多 (5)关于 (6)夕阳

4. 妾御绩纺,侍巾帷房。 纨扇圆絜,银烛炜煌。 昼眠夕寐,蓝笋象床。 弦歌酒宴,接杯举觞。 矫手顿足,悦豫且康。

5. 略

第二十二课

1. 尝 单 访

2. 详—细 持—续 恐—惧 执—行 简—单

3. (1)愿 (2)把 (3)趟

4. 嫡后嗣续,祭祀烝尝。 稽颡再拜,悚惧恐惶。 笺牒简要,顾答审详。 骸垢想浴,执热愿凉。

5. 略

第二十三课

1. 获 布 巧 任

2. 巧—妙 发—射 释—放 担—任

纷—纷 庸—俗

3. (1)获 (2)布 (3)琴 (4)任 (5)释

4. 诛斩贼盗,捕获叛亡。 布射僚丸,嵇琴阮啸。 恬笔伦纸,钧巧任钓。 释纷利俗,并皆佳妙。

5. 略

第二十四课

1. 朗 谓 领

2. 耳—环 指—甲 吸—引 佩—戴 束—缚

3. (1)指 (2)束 (3)领

4. 矩步引领,俯仰廊庙。 束带矜庄,徘徊瞻眺。 孤陋寡闻,愚蒙等诮。 谓语助者,焉哉乎也。

5. 略

附录三　本教材中华典籍汉英对照表

《春秋》　　　　　the Spring and Autumn Annals
《大学》　　　　　Great Learning
《弟子规》　　　　Di Zi Gui
《公羊传》　　　　Gong Yang Zhuan
《谷梁传》　　　　Gu Liang Zhuan
《归藏》　　　　　Guicang
《汉书》　　　　　the History of the Western Han Dynasty
《后汉书》　　　　the History of the Eastern Han Dynasty
《乐经》　　　　　the Book of Music
《礼记》　　　　　the Book of Rites
《连山》　　　　　Lianshan
《论语》　　　　　The Confucian Analects
《孟子》　　　　　Mencius
《梦溪笔谈》　　　Mengxi Bi Tan (Dream Creek Essays)
《名贤集》　　　　Ming Xian Ji (A collection of well-known and widespread Chinese sayings)
《千字文》　　　　One-Thousand-Character Essay
《儒林外史》　　　Stories of the Scholars
《三国演义》　　　the Romance of the Three Kingdoms
《三国志》　　　　the Annals of the Three Kingdoms
《三字经》　　　　Three Character Classic
《尚书》　　　　　the Book of History
《诗经》　　　　　the Book of Poetry
《史记》　　　　　Shi Ji (the Record of History)
《四书五经》　　　Four Books and Five Classics
《搜神记》　　　　Sou Shen Ji (Stories of Immortals)
《孝经》　　　　　the Classic of Filial Piety
《易经》　　　　　the Book of Changes (I Ching)

《中庸》	The Doctrine of the Mean
《周易》	Zhouyi (the Book of Changes)
《朱子家训》	Zhu Zi Jia Xun (Admonitions of Zhu Family)
《资治通鉴》	History as a Mirror
《左传》	Zuo Zhuan

附录四 One-Thousand-Character Essay

千字文

作者：周兴嗣　译者：张　杰
Author：Zhou Xingsi　Translator：Zhang Jie

天地玄黄，宇宙洪荒。
Dark sky, and yellow earth,
The universe is vast and chaotic.

日月盈昃，辰宿列张。
The sun rises and falls, the moon waxes and wanes,
Stars are orderly arranged and shine in the night sky.

寒来暑往，秋收冬藏。
Winter comes, and summer goes.
We harvest in autumn, and store in winter.

闰余成岁，律吕调阳。
Extra days in a few years make a leap month.
Music and tune balance Yin and Yang.

云腾致雨，露结为霜。
Cloud rises and turns into rain,
Waterdrops form dews and dews change into frost.

金生丽水，玉出昆冈。
Good gold comes from the Jinsha River,
Good gem is found in Mount Kunlun.

剑号巨阙，珠称夜光。
The sharpest sword is named Juque,
The most precious pearl is called Yeguang.

果珍李柰，菜重芥姜。
Plums and apples are delicious fruits,
Mustard and ginger are vital vegetables.

海咸河淡，鳞潜羽翔。
Sea water is salty, and river water is tasteless.
Finned animals swim, and winged animals fly.

龙师火帝，鸟官人皇。
Fuxi Shi is the creator of people, and Suiren Shi is the inventor of fire.
Shaohao Shi leads the Five Emperors, and Renhuang Shi rules human beings.

始制文字，乃服衣裳。
Cangjie coined Chinese characters,
Leizu clothed people.

推位让国，有虞陶唐。
Of their own accords, Shun gave up being emperor to Yao,
and Yao gave up being emperor to Yu.

吊民伐罪，周发殷汤。
Jifa of Zhou Dynasty and Chengtang of Shang Dynasty,
Attacked tyrants and brought peace to people.

坐朝问道，垂拱平章。
A good emperor could rule his empire by just sitting at court,
He would listen to his ministers politely and peace would come.

爱育黎首,臣伏戎羌。
Rulers should love and educate their people,
And neighboring people would give themselves in.

遐迩一体,率宾归王。
Far and near, all the land belonging to the king,
are peaceful and prosperous.

鸣凤在竹,白驹食场。
Phoenixes sing in the bamboo grove,
White horses graze on the grass.

化被草木,赖及万方。
Good teaching benefits grasses and trees.
It reaches the people all over the country.

盖此身发,四大五常。
The four elements① constitute our body.
The five basic virtues② make our mind.

恭惟鞠养,岂敢毁伤。
Take good care of our body,
and never dare to harm it.

女慕贞洁,男效才良。
Girls should worship women of purity and good reputation.
Boys should admire men of talents and virtue.

知过必改,得能莫忘。
Correct any mistake once learned,
And remember a trade once mastered.

---

① 四大,指四大元素,即地、水、火和风。② 五常,指仁、义、礼、智、信。

罔谈彼短，靡恃己长。
Neither talk about others' weaknesses,
Nor rely solely on your own strengths.

信使可覆，器欲难量。
Be a man of your word,
Be always broad-minded.

墨悲丝染，诗赞羔羊。
Mo Zi felt sad about the dyed silk,
The Book of Poetry spoke highly of the purity of white lambs.

景行维贤，克念作圣。
Be open and aboveboard, and act fair and square,
Overcome your selfish desires and be a saint.

德建名立，形端表正。
Good virtues shall lead to a good fame,
Good manners shall result in a good appearance.

空谷传声，虚堂习听。
Sound travels far in open valleys,
Voice becomes clear in empty halls.

祸因恶积，福缘善庆。
Wickedness invariably accumulates into misfortunes,
Goodness always leads to happiness.

尺璧非宝，寸阴是竞。
A jade of one foot is no treasure,
A split second shall not be wasted.

资父事君，曰严与敬。
Wait on our parents and serve the king,

With great care and respect.

千字文

孝当竭力，忠则尽命。
Do our best to attend our parents,
Devote our lives to the country.

临深履薄，夙兴温凊。
Be watchful in your daily life like walking on the thin ice.
Rise at dawn, wait on our parents wholeheartedly through the year.

似兰斯馨，如松之盛。
Be like the orchid, sweet and fragrant;
Be like the pine tree, upright and thriving.

川流不息，渊澄取映。
One's good deeds should be like a river, unending and flowing,
Or like water in a deep pool, clear and mirroring.

容止若思，言辞安定。
Be self-collected and behave prudently,
Stay calm and speak unhurriedly.

笃初诚美，慎终宜令。
A good start is really nice,
And a good ending is even better.

荣业所基，籍甚无竟。
With these as the foundation,
One may receive boundless honors and have a glorious life.

学优登仕，摄职从政。
Study hard and well to become an official,
Fulfill your duty and participate in political affairs.

存以甘棠，去而益咏。
Shao Gong used to work under a Gantang tree.
People kept that tree to remember him.

乐殊贵贱，礼别尊卑。
Music should cater to people's standing.
Manners should differ according to people's social status.

上和下睦，夫唱妇随。
Family members should be on good terms.
Husband and wife should live in harmony.

外受傅训，入奉母仪。
Follow your teachers' instruction abroad,
Listen to your parents' words at home.

诸姑伯叔，犹子比儿。
Treat our parents' brothers or sisters,
As if we were their sons or daughters.

孔怀兄弟，同气连枝。
Brothers should care about each other,
And be connected like branches of the same tree.

交友投分，切磨箴规。
Make friends of common interests,
Learn from and advise each other.

仁慈隐恻，造次弗离。
Love other people and be sympathetic,
Never give up these qualities whatever.

节义廉退，颠沛匪亏。
Virtues of honesty, justice, uprightness and modesty,

千字文

Should not be forgotten whenever and wherever.

性静情逸，心动神疲。
When people are composed, their minds are peaceful.
When people are tempted, their minds are disturbed.

守真志满，逐物意移。
You shall feel contented by maintaining a pure nature.
Your nature shall change when trying to satisfy your material desires.

坚持雅操，好爵自縻。
Stick to doing good and be noble,
Good luck shall come itself.

都邑华夏，东西二京。
Among cities of ancient China,
The most famous two capitals① are Luoyang and Xi'an.

背邙面洛，浮渭据泾。
Luoyang is to the south of Mount Mang and faces the Luo River.
Xi'an stands between the Wei River and the Jing River.

宫殿盘郁，楼观飞惊。
Palace buildings wind and sprawl,
Towers and pavilions are tall and flying.

图写禽兽，画彩仙灵。
In the halls are painted gods, immortals,
Flying birds and running beasts.

丙舍旁启，甲帐对楹。
On both ends, side palaces with side doors.

---

① 东京现在为河南省洛阳市；西京为陕西省西安市。

Inside, pearl screens face high pillars.

肆筵设席,鼓瑟吹笙。
With dinner tables set and seats arranged,
Musical instruments are played in such a peaceful and prosperous world.

升阶纳陛,弁转疑星。
Ministers climb up the imperial jade steps,
Their pearl-filled hats move like shining stars.

右通广内,左达承明。
Right side of the hall leads to The Hall of Guangnei①,
Left side of the hall leads to The Hall of Chengming②.

既集坟典,亦聚群英。
Guangnei houses a collection of classic books,
Chengming holds a group of talented people.

杜稿钟隶,漆书壁经。
In its collection, there are Du Du's handwriting and Zhong Yao's script,
Bamboo slips of painted scrolls and ancient classics found inside the wall in Qufu③.

府罗将相,路侠槐卿。
Inside the royal court were ministers and generals;
Outside, officials and nobles queued along both sides of the street.

户封八县,家给千兵。
Each was granted eight counties,
And protected by one thousand soldiers.

高冠陪辇,驱毂振缨。
Tall-hatted officials drove the carriage for the emperor,

---

① 广内殿,藏书处。② 承明殿,朝臣休息处。③ 曲阜,在山东,孔子故里。

They looked great with their ribbons flying high.

世禄侈富，车驾肥轻。
Their offspring were well-provided and wealthy,
They traveled in carriages with sturdy horses and light clothes.

策功茂实，勒碑刻铭。
They have made numerous achievements and contributions,
These were engraved in stone tablets and metal wares.

盘溪伊尹，佐时阿衡。
Lv Shang helped Wuwang set up the Zhou Dynasty.
Yi Yin assisted Tang in building the Shang Dynasty.

奄宅曲阜，微旦孰营。
Qufu was such a great place,
Only Zhougong could govern it.

桓公匡合，济弱扶倾。
Qi Huangong allied himself with other dukes and peace ensued;
He helped the weak and bolstered up the falling empire.

绮回汉惠，说感武丁。
Qi Liji helped Hui to be the Crown Prince and become the emperor.
Fu Yue's talents help Wuding to run the country.

俊乂密勿，多士实宁。
Thanks to the hardworking of those talents,
the country could remain peaceful and prosperous.

晋楚更霸，赵魏困横。
Jin was superseded by Chu as the most powerful overlord among the states,
Zhao and Wei were trapped by Zhang Yi's horizontal alliance.

假途灭虢，践土会盟。
Jin, making use of Yu, wiped out Guo and Yu.
Jin formed alliance with other states at Jiantu.

何遵约法，韩弊烦刑。
Xiao He made brief and clear laws and followed them.
Han Fei was punished by the numerous strict laws made by himself.

起翦颇牧，用军最精。
Bai Qi, Wang Jian, Lian Po and Li Mu,
Four famous generals most skilled in the arts of war.

宣威沙漠，驰誉丹青。
Their exploits spread far into the desert,
Their heroic stories were recorded in history.

九州禹迹，百郡秦并。
Traces of Dayu could be found all over the country.
Qin Shihuang reunified all the states into one empire.

岳宗泰岱，禅主云亭。
Mount Tai ranks first among the Five Mountains.
Emperors worshipped the earth on Mount Yun or Mount Ting.

雁门紫塞，鸡田赤城。
Only wild geese could fly past Yanmen and the Great Wall is known as Zisai,
Jitian is a fortress in the northwest and Chicheng is a gorgeous peak in Zhejiang.

昆池碣石，钜野洞庭。
Dianchi is a vast lake high in Kunming, and we can best appreciate the sea from Jieshi.
Juye and Dongting are two well-known lakes with great islands and various fishes.

千字文

旷远绵邈，岩岫杳冥。
The land of China stretches far in all directions.
There are numerous high mountains with steep cliffs and deep valleys.

治本于农，务兹稼穑。
Farming is the foundation of a country.
We must pay great attention to sowing and harvesting.

俶载南亩，我艺黍稷。
In the field facing the sun, I start farming.
I grow millet and sorghum.

税熟贡新，劝赏黜陟。
Farmers, paying taxes with newly-harvested millet, shall be praised for their good produce.
Officials shall be punished or awarded according to their performance.

孟轲敦素，史鱼秉直。
Mencius's words and deeds are always honest and sincere.
Shi Yu, an upright official historian, are always straightforward.

庶几中庸，劳谦谨敕。
People should always try to be moderate.
Hardworking, modesty, prudence and discipline are four good qualities.

聆音察理，鉴貌辨色。
When listening to others, detect their implications.
When looking at people, perceive their expressions and manners.

贻厥嘉猷，勉其祗植。
Give people good advice.
Encourage others to conduct well.

省躬讥诫,宠增抗极。
We should reflect on ourselves when being warned or mocked.
When most favors gained, beware of upcoming most disgraces.

殆辱近耻,林皋幸即。
When something dangerous or humiliating is about to come,
Quit and retire to the forest or the riverside.

两疏见机,解组谁逼。
Shu Guang and Shu Shou resigned in due time.
Nobody ever forced them to do that.

索居闲处,沉默寂寥。
Live in a remote place and stay away from any government affairs.
Maintain reticence and enjoy a peaceful life.

求古寻论,散虑逍遥。
Study ancient classics and explore ancient thoughts.
Let go all worries and live at ease.

欣奏累遣,戚谢欢招。
When happiness comes, sadness shall go away.
When worries are gone, joy shall come.

渠荷的历,园莽抽条。
Lotus flowers in the pond are in full blossom.
Trees in the garden are sprouting up.

枇杷晚翠,梧桐蚤凋。
Loquat leaves are still green in deep winter.
Phoenix trees start to wither in early autumn.

陈根委翳,落叶飘摇。
Looking down, old tree roots stretch and wind,

千字文

Looking up, leaves are falling and floating.

游鹍独运,凌摩绛霄。
Further up, a roc soars high,
Flying into the rosy clouds.

耽读玩市,寓目囊箱。
Wang Chong was poor and could only read in the market,
His attention was all on book bags and book boxes.

易輶攸畏,属耳垣墙。
After having a new light carriage, beware of the danger.
When talking, always remember that "Walls have ears".

具膳餐饭,适口充肠。
When preparing daily meals,
They should be tasty and nourishing.

饱饫烹宰,饥厌糟糠。
Even fish or meat should not be eaten when full.
Coarse food would suffice when hungry.

亲戚故旧,老少异粮。
Relatives and friends should be entertained.
The elderly and the young should have different food.

妾御绩纺,侍巾帷房。
Maids and servants should do the housework,
Wait on their masters wholeheartedly.

纨扇圆洁,银烛炜煌。
The silk fan is round and elegant.
The silvery candle is bright and brilliant.

昼眠夕寐，蓝笋象床。
When taking a nap in the day or sleep at night,
There are bamboo mats and beds decorated with ivories.

弦歌酒宴，接杯举觞。
With music being played and songs being sung,
A banquet was held and cups were raised.

矫手顿足，悦豫且康。
People sang cheerfully and danced joyfully.
They were happy and healthy.

嫡后嗣续，祭祀蒸尝。
Ancestral heritage is passed on from generation to generation.
Sacrifice should be duly offered to Heaven, Earth and ancestors.

稽颡再拜，悚惧恐惶。
We should kowtow hard repeatedly,
With sincerity, respect, fear and grief.

笺牒简要，顾答审详。
When writing a letter, it should be brief and concise.
When replying a letter, it should be detailed and clear.

骸垢想浴，执热愿凉。
One should take a bath when he gets dirty.
One wants to blow it cold when holding something hot.

驴骡犊特，骇跃超骧。
When a disaster is at hand,
Domestic animals would get frightened and run wildly.

诛斩贼盗，捕获叛亡。
Thieves, robbers, rebels and outlaws,

Must be arrested and severely punished.

布射僚丸，嵇琴阮啸。
Lv Bu helped Liu Bei with his peerless shooting;
Xiong Yiliao tossed balls to help defeat Song's army;
Ji Kang is well-known for playing Yaoqin;
Ruan Ji became enlightened while learning to whistle.

恬笔伦纸，钧巧任钓。
Meng Tian improved the writing brush;
Cai Lun innovated paper-making;
Ma Jun invented the spinning machines;
Ren Gongzi was good at fishing.

释纷利俗，并皆佳妙。
Their skills helped resolving disputes and their inventions benefited the world.
These are all wonderful and worth speaking approvingly.

毛施淑姿，工颦妍笑。
Mao Qian and Xi Shi were both beautiful and attractive.
Whether they frowned or smiled, they always looked charming.

年矢每催，曦晖朗曜。
Time, like a flying arrow, presses forward.
However, the sun always shines brightly.

璇玑悬斡，晦魄环照。
The Big Dipper[①] turns as the season changes;
The moon waxes and wanes again and again.

[①] 天璇, the second star of the Big Dipper; 天玑, the third star of the Big Dipper. The two characters together represents the Big Dipper.

指薪修祜，永绥吉劭。

Wood may burn out, but fire shall last;

People may die, but their good deeds shall be remembered forever.

矩步引领，俯仰廊庙。

With a peaceful mind, one can hold his head high and stride forward.

When looking down or up, one should behave solemnly as in a temple.

束带矜庄，徘徊瞻眺。

Be dressed decently and behave gracefully,

Be watchful and look far ahead in action.

孤陋寡闻，愚蒙等诮。

I am poorly read and ignorant.

Here is my poor writing for your criticism.

谓语助者，焉哉乎也。

My knowledge is very limited.

A few Chinese characters are all that I know.